THE ESSENTIAL GUIDE TO
BOLLYWOOD

Subhash K. Jha

Foreword by Amitabh Bachchan

Lustre Press
Roli Books

FOR SUDHIR

THE ESSENTIAL GUIDE TO
BOLLYWOOD

ISBN: 81-7436-378-5

© Roli & Janssen BV 2005
Second impression 2006
Published in India by Roli Books
in arrangement with Roli & Janssen
M-75 Greater Kailash II (Market)
New Delhi 110 048, India
Ph: ++91-11-29212271, 29212782
Fax: ++91-11-29217185.
E-mail: roli@vsnl.com; Website: rolibooks.com

Editor: Nandita Jaishankar; *Design:* Arati Subramanyam
Layout design: Kumar Raman; *Production:* Naresh Nigam

Photo Credits: National Film Archives Pune,
Private Collections, Roli Collection, Sanjay Leela Bhansali

Printed and bound in Singapore

CONTENTS

ACKNOWLEDGEMENTS

Lata Mangeshkar

Amitabh Bachchan

Jaya Bachchan

Kamal Haasan

Sanjay Leela Bhansali

Sanjeev Kohli

Simi Garewal

Jagdish Chandra Jha

Prabhavati Jha

Abhas Jha

Saroj Jha

Lata Jha

FOREWORD

Posterity interests me. And the endeavours to record for posterity interests me even more.

As a nation we have often tended to ignore a desire for systematic record keeping of the past. Historians have documented events and happenings of a nation that have been primarily related to its political bearings. But very little, or perhaps not enough, is officially known on several other aspects.

Films and entertainment is one such area. Cinema, has, through the years since its birth, been an entity rudely discarded in the social realm of this nation. Documenting any aspect of it has therefore, either been totally ignored or unthinkable.

With the passage of time and the way Indian cinema bulldozed its way into the psyche of the average citizen, it has become extremely important that we put on record aspects of this 'parallel culture', that boasts of being the largest film industry in the world and is projected by merited economists, as being one of the three top industries by the year 2020.

I am overjoyed therefore, to see the manuscript of this book *The Essential Guide to Bollywood* ... the word 'Bollywood' notwithstanding, before me and a request by my dear friend Subhash K. Jha, its author, to write its Foreword. Subhash is a journalist. A unique journalist. He writes critiques, columns, interviews, and on happenings and events connected to the film industry in Mumbai, from Patna in Bihar! His ability to stay informed and connected, almost by the hour, from such distance, is an admirable quality. And his writings appear everywhere: the national press, the locals, the colloquial, in magazines, on the net ... everywhere.

For someone with such a prolific presence in the entertainment media, it is welcoming to have him put together an exhaustive account of all that matters in the cinema industry of India.

By choosing to lead the reader through film titles, genre-wise is interesting. But following it up with a description of the film, its cast, its maker; and then doing a brief critique supported by valuable anecdotes, is brilliant. He has captured the entire relevant history of films and everything connected to it 'under one roof'.

Instead of rummaging through millions of newspapers and magazines through the years, if at all that is possible, get all you want in ... *The Essential Guide to Bollywood* by Subhash K. Jha. Well done, Subhash! My congratulations!

Posterity is valuable. Thank you for making me a part of it as well.

Amitabh Bachchan

HARMILA TAGORE
RAJESH KHANNA
SHAKTI Films
aradhana
EASTMANCOLOR
आराधना
আরাধনা

DRAMA

Andaz
1949

Cast Dilip Kumar, Raj Kapoor, Nargis, Cuckoo
Director Mehboob Khan
Music Naushad
Lyrics Majrooh Sultanpuri

The mother of all romantic triangles featuring the dream cast of Dilip Kumar, Raj Kapoor and Nargis, *Andaz* and its complexities dwelling on the man-woman relationship within the 'modern' post-Independence Indian context is, to this day, a delightful passion play. This layered study of love, passion, jealousy and tragedy showcases extraordinarily advanced camerawork by Faredoon Irani. Nargis, as rebelliously trendy as ever, plays an entrepreneur free of gender bias. Her liberal attitude, misread by her business manager (Dilip Kumar) is misconstrued as something more than friendship, and triggers off a train of dramatic events.

Awara
1951

Cast Prithviraj Kapoor, Raj Kapoor, Nargis, Leela Chitnis, Jayant
Director Raj Kapoor
Music Shankar, Jaikishan   Lyrics Shailendra

The story of a fatherless tramp Raju (Raj Kapoor) and his battle for legitimacy as he survives a fleet of social inequalities had enough twists and turns in the plot to keep the audience riveted for nearly 3 hours of passion-packed playing-time. *Awara* tells the story of a chaste woman (Leela Chitnis) falsely accused of infidelity by her husband (Prithviraj Kapoor). She is banished from her home with an unborn child who grows up to be a vagabond. The Raj Kapoor-Nargis pairing displayed dynamic daring, especially in the scene where Nargis got into a swimsuit for a mating game played out at a scale of sensuality hitherto unknown to Hindi cinema.

TIMELINE: FILMS AND LANDMARK EVENTS

1913	1918	1921	1931	1931
Raja Harishchandra	Shree Krishna Janma	Bhakta Vidur	Alam Ara	Baghban

1897

Harishchandra Sakharam Batradekar, who had a photo studio in Bombay since 1880, photographs a wrestling match in Bombay's Hanging Gardens and sends the film to London to process. The first dream of making films in India is conceived when he orders a camera for 21 guineas.

Daera

1953

Cast Meena Kumari, Nasir Khan
Director Kamal Amrohi
Music Jamal Sen
Lyrics Majrooh Sultanpuri, Kaif Bhopali

Kamal Amrohi's *Daera* is a deeply experimental look at a young and frail woman's mis-marriage with a man old enough to be her father and the suicidal fascination that her young neighbour (played by Dilip Kumar's brother Nasir Khan) develops for this silently suffering woman. The narrative constantly plays cruelly conflicting games with light and shade—deep shadows fall across the frames creating a harmony of hope and despair. *Daera* is a slight film that goes into profound areas of human relationship. Meena Kumari expressing the smothered sexuality of a lonely woman is the epitome of tragic dignity. Long before it became fashionable in cinema to borrow literary devices, *Daera* brought in a Shakespearean pathos to the story of a man's inexpressible passion in a forbidden relationship.

Awara (1951) figures in the list of the 3 most influential films in Indian cinema. *Awara* immortalized the Raj Kapoor-Nargis duo and made the blue-eyed hero the darling of the masses all the way to the former Soviet Union. Father and son Prithviraj and Raj Kapoor came together in the first of such collaborations. Shashi Kapoor (the hero's kid brother), played the childhood portion of Raj Kapoor's character.

1935	1935	1935	1936	1936
Devdas	Khoon Ka Khoon	Talas-e-Haq	Acchut Kanya	Do Diwane

1913

Dhundiraj Govind (Dadasaheb) Phalke, the father of the Indian film industry, releases the first Indian feature length film *Raja Harishchandra*.

Do Bigha Zameen
1953

Cast Balraj Sahni, Nirupa Roy, Rattan Kumar
Director Bimal Roy
Music Salil Chowdhury
Lyrics Shailendra

Arguably the most potent social drama ever conceived in this country, *Do Bigha Zameen* follows the heartrending plight of a peasant from his village. Burdened by feudal financial obligations, Shambhu (Balraj Sahni) migrates to Kolkata with his son (Rattan Kumar). As the two strangers in a cold heartless city try to find their bearings, director Bimal Roy searches out a core of humanity in the wretched conditions of the grassroot people of this land. The reverberation of Roy's treatise on socialism was far-flung and profound. Four years later, Mehboob Khan made *Mother India,* a monumental ode to peasantry. Balraj Sahni's naturalistic performance went a long way in giving the narrative a shaded and layered structure. Salil Chowdhury's arresting music borrows elements from Russian patriotic tunes and North Indian folk music.

Boot Polish
1954

Cast Baby Naaz, Rattan Kumar, David
Director Prakash Arora
Music Shankar, Jaikishan
Lyrics Shailendra

A year ahead of Satyajit Ray's Bengali masterpiece *Pather Panchali*, producer Raj Kapoor brought the neo-realism of Vittorio de Sica into mainstream Hindi cinema with *Boot Polish*. Two young actors (Baby Naaz and Rattan Kumar) play orphans left to beg on the streets by their aunt. The film's credibility emanates from the utterly natural performances by the two little actors. The fine

and now forgotten actor David as Uncle John, the do-gooder with a heart of gold, helps the two children find their bearings and learn to live with dignity. Raj Kapoor's cameo appearance on a train, where the two kids look at the blue-eyed passenger and wonder if he is *the* Raj Kapoor, reconfirmed the film's neo-realistic credentials and also evinced a smiling curiosity out of the audience.

TIMELINE: FILMS AND LANDMARK EVENTS

1937	1939	1939	1940	1941
Duniya Na Mane	Admi	Pukar	Aurat	Padosi

1914

Dadasaheb Phalke shows his first three features, *Raja Harishchandra, Mohini Bhasmasur* and *Satyavan Savitri* in London.

Cast Raj Kapoor, Nargis, Nadira
Director Raj Kapoor
Music Shankar, Jaikishan
Lyrics Shailendra, Hasrat Jaipuri

A parable on the goodness of the heart as opposed to the evil designs of the city folk, *Shri 420* features Raj Kapoor as the village bumpkin who finds out about the ways of the big bad city through his association with various characters, mainly the two women Vidya (Nargis) and Maya (Nadira) representing the 'pure' and 'corrupt' aspects of femininity. In hindsight, much of the narrative energy in this film depends on Raj Kapoor's image as the Charlie Chaplinesque hero making his way through a world of slushy machinations. The contrasts between good and bad are painstakingly recreated in sprawling studio sets. The over-elaborate climax is done as a comic outburst. The songs and dances include the classic number, *Mera joota hai japani* (sung by Mukesh to accompany Raju's tramp-like trot into the city) and the night-club number *Mud-mud ke na dekh* where the wanton Maya tries to suck Raju into a life of crime and debauchery. The romantic duet *Pyar hua ikraar hua* offers a glimpse of Raj Kapoor's three real-life children. This film served as the inspiration for many later films including Aziz Mirza's *Raju Ban Gaya Gentleman* featuring Shah Rukh Khan as a contemporary version of Raj Kapoor's character.

Boot Polish (1954) is remarkable for being the precursor to cinema about street children like Mira Nair's *Salaam Bombay* (1998), and also for the cult of ghost-direction that many illustrious filmmakers in Bollywood devised as a means of spreading their creative wings. Raj Kapoor credited the direction of this film to his assistant, Prakash Arora.

1941	1941	1942	1942	1942
Sikandar	Taj Mahal	Basant	Bharat Milap	Khandaan

1918

Indian Cinematograph Act passed providing for censorship of films and licensing of cinemas.

Devdas   1956

Cast Dilip Kumar, Suchitra Sen, Vyjanthimala, Motilal
Director Bimal Roy
Music S.D. Burman
Lyrics Sahir Ludhianvi

Bimal Roy's faithful and fiercely intimate adaptation of Saratchandra Chatterjee's classic tragedy about a self-absorbed hero who destroys his own happiness in pursuit of love, is leagues removed from P.C. Barua's minimalist version in 1935 and Sanjay Leela Bhansali's flamboyant epic in 2002. Roy's deep-focussed character study looks at Devdas Chatterjee (Dilip Kumar) as a narcissist whose self-absorbed romanticism destroys those very things that it loves, including himself. Kamal Bose's exquisite black-and-white photography captures the essence of the theme. The sordid backlanes and gullies of Kolkata are recreated with the same mellow meticulousness as the unspoilt village where Devdas and Paro grow into love. More naturalistic than stylized, Bimal Roy's *Devdas* conveys a quaint majesty in its epic thrust.

Jagte Raho   1956

Cast Raj Kapoor, Nargis, Motilal
Director Sombhu Mitra/Amit Moitra
Music Salil Chowdhury
Lyrics Shailendra, Prem Dhawan

Moving away from the operatic opulence of his style Raj Kapoor hired two avant-garde Bengali filmmakers to direct a story about one thirsty man's experiences in Kolkata during the course of one night. *Jagte Raho* is largely arresting for the utterly innovative theme and tone of narration. Raj Kapoor's encounters with various quirky, capricious and cruel characters add up to a comic and often-dark moral fable. Shot in exquisitely expressive black-and-white, the film climaxes with the celebrated sequence where Nargis, singing *Jago mohan pyare* in Lata Mangeshkar's divine voice, finally gives the tortured thirsty man his drink of water. The symbolical sequence stands out in the melee of jostling, bustling scenes that occupy the plot.

TIMELINE: FILMS AND LANDMARK EVENTS

1942	1943	1946	**1946**	1946
Muqabla	Kismet	Anmol Ghadi	**Dr Kotnis Ki Amar Kahani** (See p. 110)	Neecha Nagar

1918

Dadasaheb Phalke's Hindustan Cinema Films Co. is founded.

Do Aankhen Barah Haath   1957

Cast V. Shantaram, Sandhya
Director V. Shantaram
Music Vasant Desai
Lyrics Bharat Vyas

Like the prolific filmmaker's other humane drama *Dr Kotnis Ki Amar Kahani* made 15 years earlier with Shantaram and his real-life wife Jayshree in the lead, *Do Aankhen …* is the quasi-biographical story of a jailor (Shantaram) and his efforts to humanize six criminals. As was his wont, Shantaram shot this rugged masculine homage to humanism in the outdoors, thereby moving away from the studio-made dramas that are still the norm in mainstream Hindi cinema. The locales add considerably to the authentic mood of moral rehabilitation. The actors, especially Sandhya (the director's second wife) who is the only female presence in the plot (besides one of the prisoner's old blind mother who makes a fleeting appearance) are stylized and parabolic. Playing a toy seller who saunters into the jailor's rehabilitation plans, Sandhya's wild gesticulations in the fun-song *Chuk dhum chuk dhum* are a jolting homage to the style of acting in Marathi theatre. The famous director stepping into the hero's garb is far more restrained in expressing the anguish of an idealist.

While Bimal Roy's *Devdas* (1956) was extensively shot outdoors, every single shot in Sanjay Leela Bhansali's version of the film was shot on sets. Dilip Kumar played the first of the many Shakespearean tragic heroes of Hindi cinema. As a precursor to the 'neurotic suitor' Dilip Kumar's understated synthesis of muted machismo and finely-tuned tragedy remains a case-study of melodramatic restraint.

1948	1948	**1949**	1949	1949
Aag	Mela	**Andaz** (See p. 10)	Barsaat	Chakori

1920

Film Censor Boards are set up in four port cities: Delhi, Calcutta, Madras and Rangoon

Mother India
1957

Cast Nargis, Sunil Dutt, Raj Kumar, Rajendra Kumar, Kanhaiyalal
Director Mehboob Khan
Music Naushad
Lyrics Shakeel Badayuni

Khan's melodrama tells the rural saga of Radha (Nargis), a woman born to suffer, who rises from the ashes of ruination with a dignity and grace that exemplifies Indian womanhood. The epic begins with the old and frail Radha reliving her turbulent past with her two sons (Sunil Dutt and Rajendra Kumar) and their combined fight against feudal oppression, represented by the evil moneylender (Kanhaiyalal). Every moment is gloriously gripping, dipping in and out of the protagonist's traumatic life, first as an abandoned wife left to fend for herself and her children, then as a mother standing up for the right values.

Pyaasa
1957

Cast Guru Dutt, Mala Sinha, Waheeda Rehman, Johnny Walker, Rehman
Director Guru Dutt
Music S.D. Burman
Lyrics Sahir Ludhianvi

By far one of the most influential works of literary cinema in post-Independence India, *Pyaasa* portrays the restless poet-protagonist Vijay (Guru Dutt) as an insatiable traveller longing to find a place where his sensitivity won't be belittled. Spurned by his family, rejected by his girlfriend (Mala Sinha) who chooses to marry 'Money' (a publisher played by Rehman) Vijay finds comfort in the arms of the prostitute, Gulabo (Waheeda Rehman). *Pyaasa* represents the crest of a socially relevant cinema with enough angst to seem fiercely contemporary even now.

TIMELINE: FILMS AND LANDMARK EVENTS

1949	1949	**1949**	1950	1950
Chandni Raat	Lahore	**Mahal** (See p. 120)	Anmol Ratan	Chhoti Bhabi

1922

Entertainment tax is included in Bengal and Bombay.

Cast Dilip Kumar, Vyjanthimala, Pran, Johnny Walker
Director Bimal Roy
Music Salil Chowdhury
Lyrics Shailendra

Bimal Roy's most successful film could be deemed the mother of 'born-again' cinema with reincarnation as the main theme. The consciously kitschy tale of a beautiful village woman (Vyjanthimala) who jumps to her death to escape rape and gets justice in the next life, was written by Bengal's avant-garde filmmaker Ritwik Ghatak. Bimal Roy's chief disciple Hrishikesh Mukherjee edited the fast moving film replete with undercurrents of supernaturalism. The film got its substance mainly from the technicians and Salil Chowdhury's exceptional music score went a long way in creating an emphatically enigmatic aura around this evergreen classic. The lead pair played passionately against each other to create one of the most endearing romantic liaisons of all times.

Mehboob Khan's landmark film *Mother India* (1957) was the first Indian film to be nominated for an Oscar in the best foreign film category in 1958. Mehboob's film missed the distinction by a solitary vote at the third poll.

1950	1950	1950	**1951**	1952
Dahej	Gulnar	Jogan	**Awara** (See p. 10)	Aan

1925

Light of Asia by Himanshu Rai is the first film made as a co-production with a German company.

Dhool Ka Phool
1959

Cast Ashok Kumar Rajendra Kumar, Mala Sinha, Manmohan Krishna
Director Yash Chopra
Music N. Dutta
Lyrics Sahir Ludhianvi

Bollywood's most consistently successful director Yash Chopra's debut was a reformist drama pleading for the legitimacy of children born out of wedlock. Mala Sinha starred as a pregnant woman who is jilted by her weak lover (Rajendra Kumar). The

melodrama is memorable for its high-octave, emotionally charged performance by Mala Sinha. The triangular conflict among the unwed mother, her child's father and his wife (Nanda) was interestingly formulated.

Kaagaz Ke Phool
1959

Cast Guru Dutt, Waheeda Rehman, Veena, Baby Naaz, Johnny Walker
Director Guru Dutt
Music S.D. Burman
Lyrics Kaifi Azmi

Kaagaz Ke Phool is a mirror image of the sham and shallowness of showbiz, as seen through the eyes of the constantly anguished director Suresh Sinha (Guru Dutt) who one rainy night 'discovers' a new actress (Waheeda Rehman) and finally loses her and his happiness

to the artificial glitter of the film world. V.K. Murthy's black-and-white cinematography furnishes Dutt's melancholic treatise on life and its illusions with a sepulchral sublimity, best celebrated in the immortal song *Waqt ne kiya* (sung by the director's wife Geeta Dutt).

TIMELINE: FILMS AND LANDMARK EVENTS

1952	1952	1952	1953	1953
Aar Paar	Anhonee	Jaal	Anarkali	Baiju Bawra

1927

The world's first 'talkie' *The Jazz Singer* premieres in New York.

Cast Nutan, Sunil Dutt, Shashikala
Director Bimal Roy
Music S.D. Burman
Lyrics Majrooh Sultanpuri

Nutan and Bimal Roy gave cinema their first stunner in *Sujata*. The humanist drama about a *harijan* (untouchable) girl's fight for identity was replete with subtle sensitive touches that defied the mood of cinema in those melodramatic times. The muted stabs at social reformation were further mellowed down by Nutan's incredibly articulate performance that is now rightly regarded as a classic of shaded sentimentality. The other performances are also adequately underplayed. It is a relief beyond what mainstream cinema generally affords audience to see the protagonist's stepsister (Shashikala) portrayed as anything but a shrew. Sunil Dutt in a gallantly supportive role to the leading lady plays the man who rescues Sujata from her socially debased destiny. The film's classic numbers were sung by Lata Mangeshkar's sister Asha Bhosle.

Kaagaz Ke Phool (1959) was distinctly based on Guru Dutt's own experiences with the actress, Waheeda Rehman whom he launched and reportedly became emotionally involved with. This was the first Hindi film to be shot in cinemascope. 1959 was the year of flower power. *Dhool Ka Phool* competed for the awards with Guru Dutt's *Kaagaz Ke Phool*.

1953	**1953**	1953	**1953**	1953
Char Chand	**Daera**	Dhuan	**Do Bigha Zameen**	Footpath
	(See p. 11)		(See p. 12)	

(See p. 11) (See p. 12)

1931

Ardeshir Irani of the Imperial Film Company releases India's first full length talkie, *Alam Ara*.

Anuradha
1960

Cast Balraj Sahni, Leela Naidu, Abhi Bhattacharya
Director Hrishikesh Mukherjee
Music Pandit Ravi Shankar
Lyrics Shailendra

A progressive drama, *Anuradha*, has stood the test of time with remarkable ease. The core of the theme—what Mallika Sherawat in *Murder* 44 years later described as the abject loneliness of a married woman—is splendidly intact. Leela Naidu plays a promising singer who gives up her art to be by her village-doctor husband, Balraj Sahni's side. Soon a looming disenchantment sets in as the doctor devotes all his time caring for the sick and ill, unheedful of his own wife's wounded heart and self-worth.

Bambai Ka Babu
1960

Cast Dev Anand, Suchitra Sen
Director Raj Khosla
Music S.D. Burman
Lyrics Majrooh Sultanpuri

Bambai Ka Babu tells the dark and forbidden story of a criminal (Dev Anand) who seeks shelter in the home of a man he murders and falls in love with the murdered man's sister. Though mawkish in parts, *Bambai Ka Babu* is redeemed by the strength of the narration and the moody black-and-white cinematography by Jal Mistry. The film brings the rakish charms of Dev Anand in direct range of chemistry with Bengal's prized beauty Suchitra Sen (in one of her rare forays into Hindi cinema). Their unfulfilled love creates stirring motions of harmony within the theme of betrayal and guilt.

TIMELINE: FILMS AND LANDMARK EVENTS

1953	1953	1954	**1954**	1954
Jhansi Ki Rani	Ladki	Amar	**Boot Polish** (See p. 12)	Mirza Ghalib

1932

The Motion Picture Society of India is formed in Bombay.

Jis Desh Mein Ganga Behti Hai   1960

Cast Raj Kapoor, Padmini, Pran
Director Radhu Karmakar
Music Shankar, Jaikishan
Lyrics Shailendra, Hasrat Jaipuri

Officially directed by Raj Kapoor's regular cameraman Radhu Karmakar, the film bears the showman Raj Kapoor's imprint in every frame. The shots of the endless stretches of the ravines are awesome in their differentiation between nature and human beings. The finale of the dacoits surrendering their arms filmed to the inspiring notes of Shankar-Jaikishan's song *Aa ab laut chalen* have, to this day, the power to move us to tears. The theme of bandits under moral pressure was interspersed with a distinctly erotic romance between the simpleton reformist hero and the voluptuous bandit princess played by Padmini.

1960 was the year when Hindi cinema was in an experimental mood. Hrishikesh Mukherjee's *Anuradha* (1960) rubbed shoulders with K Asif's *Mughal-e-Azam* for audiences' attention. Dev Anand featured in 2 releases including his brother Vijay Anand's *Kala Bazaar*.

1954	1955	1955	**1955**	1956
Taxi Driver	Devdas	Mr and Mrs 55	**Shree 420** (See p. 14)	Chori Chori

1933

Himanshu Rai's *Karma*, starring Devika Rani premieres in London. The passionate kissing sequence sparks controversy.

Mughal-e-Azam   1960

Cast Prithiviraj Kapoor, Dilip Kumar, Madhubala,
    Durga Khote, Ajit
Director K. Asif
Music Naushad
Lyrics Shakeel Badayuni

Flawless, seamless and timeless, *Mughal-e-Azam* immortalized each one of its cast members and technicians. Its imposing grandeur, breathtaking beauty and, most importantly, its emotional energy within its imposing visuals, remain undimmed by the tides of time as an imperishable classic with a contemporary narrative. Each frame exudes the aroma of priceless nostalgia. With every generation the verbal sparring between Emperor Akbar (Prithiviraj Kapoor) and his adamant son Salim (Dilip Kumar) acquires renewed poetic intensity, thanks in no small measure to the dialogues which fall in a tumult of pride, honour and self identity into Asif's epic design. The opulence of the sets, the regal bearing of the characters, their splendid yet subdued expressions and articulations refuse to become a *kaneez* (slave) to passing fads, fancies and trends. From the first frame to the last, the intensity of the lovers' passion infects the audience like no other romantic epic. Dilip Kumar's understated expressions of romantic passion are, to this day, exemplary. R.D. Mathur's cinematography was far ahead of its time, panning the lovers' faces and the breathtaking landscape with equal grace. The symmetry of time and space achieved within the restrictions imposed by the period genre that demands a strictly melodramatic mode of execution, are a marvel of disciplined creativity. As Madhubala sings, dances, suffers and perishes for love, we wonder if there can ever be another epitome of beauty quite like her, or if another film can do justice to someone as beautiful as Madhubala!

TIMELINE: FILMS AND LANDMARK EVENTS

1956	1956	1957	1957	1957
CID	**Jagte Raho** (See p. 14)	Bhabhi	**Do Aankhen Barah Haath** (See p. 15)	**Mother India** (See p. 16)

1935

P.C. Barua's *Devdas* starring K.L. Saigal and Jamuna is a huge success and becomes a reference point in Hindi cinema.

Ganga Jumna

1961

DRAMA

23

Cast Dilip Kumar, Vyjanthimala, Nasir Khan

Director Nitin Bose

Music Naushad

Lyrics Shakeel Badayuni

The conflict between two brothers became a favourite part of Hindi cinema's formulaic lexicon. But none was as splashy and dramatic as *Gunga Jumna* (1961). Dilip Kumar, who holds up the film's flamboyant frames with his winsome and crowd-pleasing Awadhi language and rustic mannerisms, is said to have ghost-directed this film.

Dilip Kumar pulled out all the stops to play the outlawed Ganga who moves from the village into the jungles after being persecuted by the resident *zamindar* (landowner). To create an ironic suspense, the film puts the dacoit's brother Jumna (Dilip Kumar's real-life sibling Nasir Khan) on the crime route. There was sibling rivalry and there was romantic revelry. The film works both as a romance and drama of breached brotherhood.

1957	1957	**1957**	1957	**1958**
Musafir	Naya Daur	**Pyaasa** (See p. 16)	Tumsa Nahin Dekha	**Chalti Ka Naam** **Gaadi** (See p. 98)

1935

Himanshu Rai, director of *Light of Asia* (1925), sets up Bombay Talkies.

Sahib Bibi Aur Ghulam 1962

Cast Meena Kumari, Guru Dutt, Waheeda Rehman
Director Abrar Alvi
Music Hemant Mukherjee
Lyrics Shakeel Badayuni

Sahib Bibi Aur Ghulam, adapted from Bimal Mitra's Bengali novel tells the story of the haunted and desperately lonely daughter-in-law of a feudal family in the 19th century who refuses to become an adornment in the ancestral mansion. Choti Bahu (played by Meena Kumari) leaves an everlasting impression of tragic grace. Rebellious, hysterical, passionate and doomed, this is the actress's most celebrated performance along with *Pakeezah*. As a captivating counterpoint to Meena Kumari's doomed glory, there is Waheeda Rehman as the impish Zabaa, singing coltishly in Asha Bhosle's voice. Caught between the two essential faces of femininity is Bhoothnath (Guru Dutt) whose reverent adoration of his *maalkin* (employer) and indulgent fondness for the girl next door provide the plot with an exceptional resonance.

Bandini 1963

Cast Ashok Kumar, Nutan, Dharmendra
Director Bimal Roy
Music S.D. Burman
Lyrics Shailendra, Gulzar

Chronicling the passionate story of the imprisoned Kalyani through Kamal Bose's expressive black-and-white photography, Roy takes us into a formidable flashback filled with the sound and fury of the Indian Freedom Movement in the 1930s. Amidst the turmoil of rebellion Kalyani (Nutan) falls in love with the revolutionary Bikas (Ashok Kumar). Many years later Kalyani runs into her lover, now married to a shrew. The film's supremely celebrated climax has Kalyani making the toughest decision of any woman's life. *Bandini* is one of the most poignant tales of love during stressful times ever told in Hindi cinema. Bimal Roy's revolutionary vision lanced across the frames giving the narrative a poetic vision.

TIMELINE: FILMS AND LANDMARK EVENTS

1958	**1958**	1959	1959	**1959**
Kala Pani	**Madhumati** (See p. 17)	Anari	Ardhangini	**Dhool Ka Phool** (See p. 18)

1935

The first All India Motion Picture Convention is held in Bombay.

Mere Mehboob

1963

Cast Ashok Kumar, Sadhana, Rajendra Kumar, Nimmi
Director H.S. Rawail
Music Naushad
Lyrics Shakeel Badayuni

Mere Mehboob is a love triangle set within a decadent aristocratic Muslim ambience, and is the best known example of the archaic genre known as the 'Muslim Social.' It is a painstakingly put together ritual of courtship filled with garish sets and ornate dialogues denoting a sense of renewed nostalgia associated with a defunct 'Nawabi' culture. During the same decade Guru Dutt also attempted a similar Muslim love triangle *Chaudhvin Ka Chand* with considerable success, though the success of *Mere Mehboob*, thanks to Naushad's innumerable love songs including the hit title song *Mere mehboob tujhe meri mohabbat ki kasam* and *Mere mehboob mein kya nahin*, remains unique to the genre. The film immortalized Sadhana's beauty and grace, elevating her to the status of a minor icon for a while.

Interestingly Meena Kumari was the first and only choice for the role of Choti Bahu in *Sahib Bibi Aur Ghulam* (1962). For the male protagonist's part Guru Dutt wanted Dilip Kumar. When he failed to turn up the director took on the character. Because of the director's personal proximity to the actress, singer Geeta Dutt refused to sing for Waheeda Rehman.

1959	1959	**1959**	**1959**	**1960**
Dil Deke Dekho	Ghar Ghar Ki Baat	**Kagaz Ke Phool** (See p. 18)	**Sujata** (See p. 19)	**Anuradha** (See p. 20)

(See p. 18) (See p. 19) (See p. 20)

1935

The first trade journal is started by the Motion Picture Society of India.

Mujhe Jeene Do

Cast Sunil Dutt, Waheeda Rehman
Director Moni Bhattacharya
Music Jaidev
Lyrics Sahir Ludhianvi

Sunil Dutt produced and played the lead in this pioneering dacoit drama. Like Nitin Bose's *Ganga Jumna* and Raj Kapoor's *Jis Desh Mein Ganga Behti Hai*—the two other famous dacoit dramas of the 1960s—*Mujhe Jeene Do* pitches its passionate plea at a socially conscious level. The central plot about the seismic romance between the dacoit Sunil Dutt and the prostitute played by Waheeda Rehman is played out at an intensely lyrical pitch. The two social outcastes' efforts to set up a home and ensure a safe future for their child makes for a poignant drama, heightened by Sahir's poetry and Jaidev's music. Lata Mangeshkar singing *Tere bachpan ko jawani ki dua deti hoon* is particularly expressive of the film's plea to let every individual live with dignity.

TIMELINE: FILMS AND LANDMARK EVENTS

1960	1960	**1960**	1960	**1960**
Bambai Ka Babu (See p. 20)	Chaudhvin Ka Chand	**Jis Desh Mein Ganga Behti Hai** (See p. 21)	Kala Bazaar	**Mughal-e-Azam** (See p. 22)

1936

Ardeshir Irani of the Imperial Film Company sets up a cinecolour processing laboratory.

Cast Sushil Kumar, Sudhir Kumar
Director Satyen Bose
Music Laxmikant, Pyarelal
Lyrics Majrooh Sultanpuri

This mega money-spinner for the Rajshri banner featured completely untried faces, not just in the lead but also at the periphery where Sanjay Khan appeared in a romantic sub-plot. But the main plot featured two unknown actors Sushil Kumar and Sudhir Kumar as physically challenged friends struggling to survive with dignity in the concrete jungle. There was only one star in this roaring hit. And that was Laxmikant-Pyarelal's music. Though designed as a commercial drama, *Dosti* broke several rules of mainstream cinema. Like Satyen Bose's other films (*Chalti Ka Naam Gadi, Jeevan Mrityu, Bandish, Aasra* and *Mere Bhaiya*) bonds that take individuals beyond family ties were very important to *Dosti*. The film celebrated the theme of friendship in a language that remains relevant and desirable to this day.

Sunil Dutt's breakthrough came with Mehboob Khan's magnum opus, *Mother India* (1957). Dutt turned producer in the 1960s with a series of off-beat films (*Mujhe Jeene Do,*1963 *Yeh Raste Hai Pyar Ke*, 1963), which only added to his reputation and commercial standing.

1961	1961	1961	1961	1962
Ganga Jumna	**Hum Dono**	Jab Pyar Kisi Se	Junglee	Asli Naqli
(See p. 23)	(See p. 110)	Hota Hai		

1937

The Indian Motion Pictures Producers' Association is founded in Bombay.

Sangam 1964

Cast Raj Kapoor, Vyjanthimala, Rajendra Kumar
Director Raj Kapoor
Music Shankar, Jaikishan
Lyrics Shailendra, Hasrat Jaipuri

In his first colour film, Raj Kapoor went kitschy with a captivating vengeance to tell the story of three childhood friends Gopal (Kumar), Sundar (Kapoor) and Radha (Vyjanthimala). Radha loves Gopal but Sundar, pushy and naïve as only Raj Kapoor can be, refuses to see the writing on the wall. The lavishly mounted film takes the trio through a tumultuous round-the-world trip until the triangle is finally resolved with Gopal's suicide. The film's arresting song sequences shot in over-saturated colours suggests a festive flamboyant flair for melodrama and escapism. Raj Kapoor had originally called the film *Gharonda* and wished to cast Dilip Kumar in the role of Gopal.

Aakhri Khat 1966

Cast Master Bunty, Rajesh Khanna, Indrani Mukherjee
Director Chetan Anand
Music Khayyam
Lyrics Kaifi Azmi

A minor masterpiece from Rajesh Khanna's pre-superstardom phase, *Aakhri Khat* stars an infant Master Bunty who is left on the streets to fend for himself after his mother (Indrani Mukherjee) dies, leaving the little boy to his own devices. Jal Mistry's skillful camera careens through the little boy's scary adventures in the concrete jungle as he moves from place to place in search of comfort and grace. This is an unbelievably natural performance by the little boy, buoyed by a haunting music score by Khayyam. Two melodies *Baharon mera jeevan bhi sawaron* and *Mere chanda* (the latter poignantly expressing the helplessness of the dead mother to comfort her wandering child) by Lata Mangeshkar have stood the test of time. So has this unusual film from a versatile director.

TIMELINE: FILMS AND LANDMARK EVENTS

1962	1962	1962	1962	1962
Baat Ek Raat Ki	Bees Saal Baad	China Town	Ek Musafir Ek Hasina	Hariyali Aur Raasta

1937

Ardeshir Irani of the Imperial Film Company releases the first colour film, *Kisan Kanya*.

Anupama

Cast Dharmendra, Sharmila Tagore, Tarun Bose, Shashikala, Deven Varma
Director Hrishikesh Mukherjee
Music Hemant Kumar
Lyrics Kaifi Azmi

A mute and minimalist drama far ahead of its times, *Anupama* tells the story of Uma (Sharmila Tagore) whose father (played with brilliant authority by Tarun Bose) detests his daughter ever since his beloved wife died during childbirth. The transference of his grief into the daughter's guilt is majestically achieved through the subtle

screenplay and sparse dialogues. Dharmendra as an author who brings the repressed girl's angst out is also unforgettable. The stress on the spoken word and its opposition to

Sharmila Tagore and Tarun Bose were subconscious precursors to Aishwarya Rai and Amitabh Bachchan in Aditya Chopra's *Mohabbatein* (2000).

the silence of stifled emotions comes across in the contrasting characters played by Sharmila Tagore and Shashikala. What gave *Anupama* its bedrock of emotional strength was the troubled father-daughter relationship.

1962	1962	**1962**	1963	**1963**
Kala Samunder	Professor	**Sahib Bibi Aur Ghulam** (See p. 24)	Bahurani	**Bandini** (See p. 24)

1938

The Indian film industry celebrates its Silver Jubilee.

Devar

1966

Cast Dharmendra, Sharmila Tagore, Deven Varma, Shashikala
Director Mohan Segal
Music Roshan
Lyrics Anand Bakshi

The compelling quadrangular melodrama about a mismatched couple contained deep elements of Bengali literature. Stress within the domestic ambience was created when the noble Dharmendra ends up marrying the shrewish Shashikala while his brother contrives to marry the virtuous and beautiful Sharmila Tagore. The film is remarkable for projecting the ironic twists of fate in an unconventional format with the lead pair bound to the 'wrong' spouses till the very end. When the truth is revealed (Dharmendra and Sharmila were childhood sweethearts) it's too late to turn back.

Guide

1966

Cast Dev Anand, Waheeda Rehman, Leela Chitnis, Anwar Husain, Kishore Sahu
Director Vijay Anand
Music S.D. Burman
Lyrics Shailendra

Vijay Anand smoothly recreates R.K. Narayan's complex and layered novel, and mixes existentialism with the song-and-dance formula. Waheeda Rehman comes to life as the capricious, defiant and enchanting Rosy, and Dev Anand is every bit Raju Guide who goes from guiding tourists in Rajasthan to guiding the much-married Rosy out of a suffocating marriage into a super-career as a dancer. In the last lap of this fascinating and beguiling drama of love, deception and redemption, Dev Anand is transformed into a saint, the saviour of a drought-stricken village. Rehman, in her best role had Lata Mangeshkar's voice making Rosy a ravishing mirror of enigma and emancipation.

TIMELINE: FILMS AND LANDMARK EVENTS

1963	**1963**	**1963**	1963	1963
Gumraah (See p. 114)	**Mere Mehboob** (See p. 25)	**Mujhe Jeene Do** (See p. 26)	Sanjh Aur Savera	Tere Ghar Ke Samne

1940

The Film Advisory Board is set up in Bombay.

Mamta

Cast Ashok Kumar, Suchitra Sen, Dharmendra
Director Asit Sen
Music Roshan
Lyrics Majrooh Sultanpuri

Remaking his own 1963 Bengali hit *Uttar Phalguni*, Asit Sen does a searing sentimental pilgrimage into the anatomy of motherhood with the mythic Suchitra Sen cast as both mother and daughter. In true *Mother India* tradition, the mother sacrifices all happiness and comfort to see her daughter grow up with dignity. The flickering images of the martyr's slow fade-out is manifested in Sen's over-done melodramatic performance controlled and set to a compelling pitch by Lata Mangeshkar's songs *Rehte the kabhi jinke dil mein* and the imperishable *Rahen na rahen hum*. The film shows remarkable sensitivity and maturity in portraying the relationship between the mother and the man who would

have been her husband (Ashok Kumar). It's from the Sen-Kumar sequences that this melodrama gets its great emotional power.

Far ahead of its times, and as timeless in its emotional and dramatic resonances as the voice of Lata Mangeshkar which guides Rosy to glory, *Guide* (1966) is a multifaceted work of popular art with a music score by S.D. Burman that ranks as one of the 10 all-time bests.

1964	**1964**	1964	**1964**	1964
Ayee Milan Ki Bela	**Dosti** (See p. 27)	Geet Gaya Pattharon Ne	**Haqeeqat** (See p. 111)	Kashmir Ki Kali

1940

Himanshu Rai, founder of Bombay Talkies, passes away.

Phool Aur Patthar
1966

Cast Meena Kumari, Dharmendra, Shashikala, O.P. Ralhan
Director: O.P. Ralhan
Music Ravi   **Lyrics** Shakeel Badayuni

Anoteworthy potboiler depicting a forbidden liaison between a widow (Meena Kumari) and a petty criminal (Dharmendra). The sequence in which Dharmendra crept up to the supine heroine in a shirtless, drunken stupor had audiences whistling in delight. The screenplay blended the elements of a typical entertainer with a strong social comment on widow remarriage. The assertive vamp (Shashikala) provided a persuasive counterpoint to the chaste and inviolable widow. It was by far the most fruitful collaborative effort of Dharmendra and Meena Kumari during their much talked-about friendship in the 1960s.

Teesri Kasam
1966

Cast Raj Kapoor, Waheeda Rehman
Director Basu Bhattacharya
Music Shankar, Jaikishan
Lyrics Shailendra, Hasrat Jaipuri

Basu Bhattacharya's directorial debut, *Teesri Kasam* adapts litterateur Phanishwarnath Renu's novel about the bond that grows between a simple-hearted bullock-cart driver (Raj Kapoor) and the professional dancer (Waheeda Rehman) who visits his village. Bhattacharya focussed on the feelings underlining the two characters' relationship rather than the star-value afforded by the cast. Brilliantly shot in black-and-white by Nabendu Ghosh, *Teesri Kasam* features a number of memorabilia sung by Mukesh. *Teesri Kasam* is today regarded as Kapoor's most credible rendering of his simpleton's image that became caricatural in the 1970s with films like *Diwana* and *Sapnon Ka Saudagar*.

TIMELINE: FILMS AND LANDMARK EVENTS

1964	**1964**	1964	1965	1965
Kohraa	**Sangam**	Suhagan	Bahu Beti	Bedaag
(See p. 120)	(See p. 28)			

1942

Shortage in raw film and equipment restricts the length of film to conserve stock for war propaganda films.

Cast Shammi Kapoor, Asha Parekh, Premnath, Helen
Director Vijay Anand
Music R.D. Burman
Lyrics Majrooh Sultanpuri

Shammi Kapoor's rebellious 'yahoo' in *Junglee* (1961) exemplified the swinging sixties. His acting, dancing and dress style, (a mix of James Dean and Elvis Presley) made him a cult figure amongst the youth.

Blending producer Nasir Husain's trademark formula of frolic and romance with director Vijay Anand's penchant for using song, dance and drama as extensions of the characters' inner world, *Teesri Manzil* created a storm at the box office. The plot is a murder mystery about a girl befriending a musician at a hill station to find out the identity of her sister's killer. Much of the plot seems an excuse for Burman's rousing songs rendered with glorious gusto by Mohammad Rafi and Asha Bhosle. In his first major tryst with the hit parade, Burman created smash-hit tracks like *O mere sona re, O haseena zulfon wali, Aaja aaja main hoon pyar tera* and the uncharacteristically sober Rafi solo *Tumne mujhe dekha* which was filmed immediately after the leading man's wife Geeta Bali passed away. One of the lead pair's biggest hits, Kapoor and Parekh somehow failed to click together in subsequent projects like *Jawan Mohabbat* and *Pagla Kahin Ka*.

1965	1965	1965	1965	1965
Bheegi Raat	Bhoot Bangla	Chand Aur Suraj	Chupa Rustom	Janam Janam Ke Saathi

1942

Filmistan Studio, a rival to Bombay Talkies, is set up by Shashadhar Mukherjee, Gyan Mukherjee, Rai Bahadur Chunilal and Ashok Kumar.

Milan

1967

Cast Nutan, Sunil Dutt, Jamuna, Deven Varma
Director A. Subba Rao
Music Laxmikant, Pyarelal
Lyrics Anand Bakshi

A rare success on the theme of reincarnation, *Milan* was very different from the other success in the genre, *Madhumati*. Telling the tale of forbidden love between a simple boatman (Dutt) and a classy woman from an aristocratic family (Nutan) the Telugu director (making his debut in Hindi) took us on location to a fisher village to shoot the stirring love tale. The film opens with the newly married couple discovering their togetherness in several previous lives through the hit song *Hum tum yug-yug se yeh geet milan ke*. Laxmikant-Pyarelal's songs contributed immensely to the film's popularity. The lead pair was brilliantly underplayed, especially in the scenes depicting the heroine's widowhood and the boatman's efforts to console her. The South Indian actress Jamuna made a rare appearance in a Hindi film as the over-possessive third angle in the love triangle.

Raat Aur Din

1967

Cast Nargis, Pradeep Kumar, Feroz Khan
Director Satyen Bose
Music Laxmikant, Pyarelal
Lyrics Shankar, Jaikishan

A rare attempt to delve into a psychologically complex theme, *Raat Aur Din* featured Nargis in her last performing role, as a schizophrenic representing the two aspects of darkness (*raat*) and light (*din*). There was certain sensitivity in the narration that director Bose achieved through Nargis' extremely credible performance. She got terrific support from singer Lata Mangeshkar whose numbers *Awaara ae mere dil* and *Na chedo kal ke afsane, Dil ki girah khol do* went a long way in creating an aura of enigma and apprehension around the central character. Nargis had married and retired from cinema by the time this film was released. She received the National Award for her performance that recalled her earlier day-and-night star-turn in K.A. Abbas' 1952 psycho-drama *Anhonee*.

TIMELINE: FILMS AND LANDMARK EVENTS

1965	1965	1966	1966	1966
Janwar	Waqt	**Aakhri Khat** (See p. 28)	**Anupama** (See p. 29)	**Devar** (See p. 30)

1942

Directors V. Shantaram, Mehboob Khan and A.R. Kardar set up their independent film production units.

Anokhi Raat

Cast Sanjeev Kumar, Zaheeda, Parikshat Sahni, Aruna Irani
Director Asit Sen
Music Indivar
Lyrics Roshan

A modernistic chamber piece about a group of people who huddle together under unlikely though not impossible circumstances during one story night. Sanjeev Kumar plays an outlaw who believes the woman in the present is his dead wife from the past. Legendary actress Nargis' niece Zaheeda made her debut in the challenging double role. Director Asit Sen (not to be confused with the comic actor of the same name) captured the desperately driven people

trapped under one roof with an intensity that defined the moment as well as the feelings and emotions which underscored their interaction. *Anokhi Raat*—Sen's experimental best— extracted exquisitely neo-realistic performances from the entire cast who had to be both cinematic and authentic to fulfill the director's double vision of an ordinary world driven by extraordinary circumstances. Composer Roshan's music was an asset. The film's best-known song, *Mehlon ka raja mila,* sung with soul-piercing poignancy by Lata Mangeshkar was recorded by the composer's wife Ira Roshan after his death.

Through the 1960s and '70s, Nutan picked up awards for multifarious roles in films like *Milan* (1967), *Saraswatichandra* (1969) and *Main Tulsi Tere Aangan Ki* (1978). Till the 1980s she maintained her preeminence, acting for the first time opposite Dilip Kumar in *Karma* (1986).

1966	**1966**	1966	**1966**	**1966**
Dil Diya Dard Liya	**Guide** (See p. 30)	Love in Tokyo	**Mamta** (See p. 31)	**Phool Aur Patthar** (See p. 32)

1943

Government imposes control on supply of raw film.

Ashirwad
1968

Cast Ashok Kumar, Sanjeev Kumar,
Sumita Sanyal, Veena
Director Hrishikesh Mukherjee
Music Vasant Desai
Lyrics Gulzar

In an author-backed central role of a poet married to a female *zamindar* (Veena—stern and stoic), Ashok Kumar (in a National Award winning performance) created a character that was at once soft, sensitive and stubborn. The epic screenplay was a spiral of calamitous circumstances strung together by the hands of a master storyteller. Reversing the matriarchal rules of cinematic melodrama, Mukherjee created one of Hindi cinema's most powerful treatise on the special father-daughter relationship. *Ashirwad* is Mukherjee's most elegiac film ever. Standing tall at the centre of this remarkably rich emotional tale is Ashok Kumar whose incredibly prolonged career as a leading man climaxed with this film. The actor made us forget the external aberrations to take us on an unforgettable emotional journey. His self-rendered *Rail gadi rail gadi* sung in a park full of frolicking children displayed Ashok Kumar's proclivity to be the consummate mass entertainer.

Sangharsh
1968

Cast Dilip Kumar, Vyjanthimala, Balraj Sahni,
Jayant, Sanjeev Kumar
Director H.S. Rawail
Music Naushad
Lyrics Shakeel Badayuni

A blood-and-thunder tale about a cult of outlaws, *Sangharsh* was raised to an extraordinary cinematic experience by the stunning ensemble cast of formidable actors. Dilip Kumar of course rose to dramatic heights in both his dramatic and lighter moments in the narrative. Others including Jayant playing Kumar's bloodthirsty grandfather and Balraj Sahni were exceptionally attuned to the violent mood of Bengali litterateur Mahashweta Devi's original novel. Though she was unhappy with the screen adaptation, Rawail brought a ravishing resonance to the drama.

TIMELINE: FILMS AND LANDMARK EVENTS

1966	**1966**	1967	**1967**	**1967**
Teesri Kasam	**Teesri Manzil**	An Evening In Paris	**Jewel Thief**	**Milan**
(See p. 32)	(See p. 33)		(See p. 121)	(See p. 34)

1943

India's first certified blockbuster *Kismet* opens and runs for four uninterrupted years in a theatre in Calcutta.

Cast Nutan, Manish, Ramesh Deo
Director Govind Saraiya
Music Kalyanji, Anandji
Lyrics Indivar

A rare thematically and creatively correct adaptation of a literary work, *Saraswatichandra* is an elaborate critique of social norms in the 19th century. We see the two protagonists Saraswatichandra

(Manish) and Kumud (Nutan) caught between tradition and reform as their life is tossed from one level of torment to another. Unable to unite, the two protagonists are caught in various states of estrangement defined by a distending socio-cultural drama. Kumud who is in many vital ways the more important protagonist falls into a marital misalliance. After widowhood she renounces the chance to finally marry her true love. The music and the vocals (by Lata Mangeshkar and Mukesh) lift the epic tale to heights of glory and grandiosity. One of Bollywood's abiding musical hits, *Saraswatichandra* is further elevated by Nutan's strongly resonant central performance. Like Sanjay Leela Bhansali many decades later, Govind Saraiya's literary adaptation showed a skilled sensitivity and splendour absent in many other films made from literature.

Ashok Kumar's lucky break came in 1935 when Nazmul Hussein, the hero of Himanshu Rai's *Jeevan Naiyya* (1936) disappeared four days before shooting. Ashok, then serving as Rai's lab assistant, replaced Nazmul. The film was a hit and Ashok was immensely appreciated. He never looked back.

1967	1967	1968	1968	1968
Raat Aur Din	**Ram Aur Shyam**	**Ashirwad**	Ankhen	**Anokhi Raat**
(See p. 34)	(See p. 98)	(See p. 36)		(See p. 35)

1944

Dadasaheb Phalke, the father of the Indian film industry, who had released India's first film, *Raja Harishchandra* (1913), passes away.

Aradhana   1969

Cast Ashok Kumar, Sharmila Tagore, Rajesh Khanna,
Farida Jalal, Madan Puri, Anita Guha, Manmohan,
Pahadi Sanyal
Director Shakti Samanta
Music S.D. Burman
Lyrics Anand Bakshi

The consummate masala-melodrama launched Rajesh Khanna as Bollywood's first superstar, and also established Kishore Kumar as India's no.1 male playback singer. The ghost-voice played an unquestionable role in rolling in the Khanna mania. The minute Kishore sang *Mere sapnon ki rani* for Khanna the nation went into a collective swoon. Ironically

Aradhana wasn't Khanna's author-backed film! Although he played both father and son, it was Sharmila Tagore as the unwed mother struggling to bring up her illegitimate offspring in a brutally cold, harsh and uncaring world who held the show together with her performance. S.D. Burman's musical score vastly and vigorously supported the remarkable melodrama. The seduction song *Roop tera mastana* where the coy unmarried girl is impregnated was done in one take. Khanna with his unbuttoned shirt and Tagore in a flaming–red blanket set the screen on fire.

TIMELINE: FILMS AND LANDMARK EVENTS

1968	1968	1968	1968	1968
Brahmachari	Dil Aur Mohabbat	Do Kaliyan	Farishta	Kanyadaan

1945

Control on the distribution of raw film stock is removed.

Do Raaste

1969

Cast Rajesh Khanna, Mumtaz, Balraj Sahni, Prem Chopra, Bindu,
Kamini Kaushal, Jayant

Director Raj Khosla

Music Laxmikant, Pyarelal

Lyrics Anand Bakshi

Though more recognized for his classic performance in *Do Bigha Zameen* and *Garam Hawa*, Balraj Sahni was equally credible and compelling in this film as the noble and suffering patriarch of a joint family who dedicates his life to looking after his two stepbrothers (Prem Chopra and Rajesh Khanna), only to have one of them turn against him when Chopra marries a shrew. The popular vamp of the 1970s Bindu made a piercing impact as the conniving daughter-in-law who weans her husband away from his family. Based on a well-known Gujarati novel, *Do Raaste* boasted of powerful dramatic content and one of the composing duo Laxmikant-Pyarelal's most successful music scores ever. Chart-busting songs like *Chup gaye saare nazaare, Yeh reshmi zulfein, Mere naseeb mein ae dost* and *Bindiya chamkegi* (one of the biggest hits of the decade) gave the roomy plot a chance to develop the Khanna-Mumtaz romance.

Sharmila Tagore wasn't producer-director Shakti Samanta's first choice for *Aradhana* (1969). After Aparna Sen chickened out at the prospect of playing mom to the hero in her (and his) prime, Tagore bravely applied chalk to her lustrous tresses, abandoned the trademark bouffant and sequined saris for the widow's weeds in the second-half, and gave an award-winning performance.

1968	**1968**	1968	**1968**	1968
Mere Huzoor	**Padosan** (See p. 99)	Sadhu Aur Shaitan	**Sangharsh** (See p. 36)	Sapnon Ka Saudagar

1946

Chetan Anand's *Neecha Nagar is* shown at the Cannes Film Festival.

Khamoshi

1969

Cast Waheeda Rehman, Rajesh Khanna, Dharmendra, Deven Varma, Lalita Pawar

Director Asit Sen

Music Hemant Mukherjee   **Lyrics** Gulzar

An exquisite expression of subliminal psychological desires with the timeless Waheeda Rehman cast as a nurse in a mental hospital whose emotions are used to cure traumatized patients; first Dharmendra then Rajesh Khanna. The pressure of serving as a guinea pig finally takes its toll on the healer who ends up as a patient in her own psychiatric ward. *Khamoshi* plays a peculiarly poignant game of light-and-shade with the female protagonist's character.

Satyakam

1969

Cast Dharmendra, Sharmila Tagore, Sanjeev Kumar

Director Hrishikesh Mukherjee

Music Laxmikant, Pyarelal

Lyrics Kaifi Azmi

This immensely satisfying film remains an abiding favourite. An absolutely natural performance by Dharmendra portrays the life of Satyapriya, an idealistic engineer whose dreams of a free, morally liberated India turn sour. He redeems his conscience by marrying a 'fallen woman' Ranjana (Tagore) and adopting her illegitimate child. Decades after it was made, *Satyakam* remains a pertinent and acutely conscientious mirror of Independent India's soured yearnings. Rajinder Singh Bedi's scathing dialogues and the director's ability to create drama without going overboard gives the narrative a cutting edge.

TIMELINE: FILMS AND LANDMARK EVENTS

1968	1969	1969	1969	1969
Saraswatichandra	**Aradhana**	**Do Raaste**	**Ittefaq**	**Khamoshi**
(See p. 37)	(See p. 38)	(See p. 39)	(See p. 122)	(See p. 40)

Saraswatichandra (See p. 37) — Aradhana (See p. 38) — Do Raaste (See p. 39) — Ittefaq (See p. 122) — Khamoshi (See p. 40)

1947

A landmark in Indian history. On 15th August, India wins Independence from the British.

Dastak

1970

Cast Rehana Sultan, Sanjeev Kumar
Director Rajinder Singh Bedi
Music Madan Mohan
Lyrics Majrooh Sultanpuri

Urdu–Hindi litterateur Rajinder Singh Bedi turned director with this skilled and layered look at the housing problem in Mumbai and a crumbling marriage between a Muslim couple, salvaged and finally sublimated by the music in their souls. *Dastak* is the first Hindi film to look at Muslims as mainstream people. Sanjeev Kumar plays the ordinary working-class guy Hamid while Salma is his new burqa-less bride. They move into a house of disrepute where a prostitute once lived. Rehana Sultan portrays the transformation of the timid devoted housewife into a psychologically disturbed woman traumatized by the erotic ghosts that haunt her new home. Sultan played the role with subtle skills and even won the prestigious National Award for it. Far ahead of its time in theme and treatment, *Dastak* was path-breaking drama in the truest sense.

In *Khamoshi* (1969) Dharmendra is only captured in silhouettes—his face is not visible to the camera. Director Asit Sen, who went on to make several psychologically dense mainstream films, got great help for this particular film from Hemant Mukherjee's music compositions.

1969	**1969**	1970	1970	1970
Saat Hindustani	**Satyakam** (See p. 40)	Dastak	Johnny Mera Naam	Kati Patang

---

1947

The Partition of India reshuffles the population and the film industry. Bombay (in India) becomes the biggest film-production centre; Calcutta (India) makes regional films. The film industry in Lahore (now in Pakistan) is shattered.

Khilona

1970

Cast Sanjeev Kumar, Mumtaz, Jeetendra, Shatrughan Sinha
Director Chandar Vohra
Music Laxmikant, Pyarelal
Lyrics Anand Bakshi

The illustrious producer L.V. Prasad specialized in potboilers with a heart of gold. In this interesting adaptation of pulp novelist Gulshan Nanda's bestseller, Prasad played puppeteer to director Chandar Vohra to tell a melodramatic story of a prostitute (Mumtaz) and a clinically insane man (Sanjeev Kumar). The prostitute is brought to the 'respectable' household to heal the hero. Once cured, he forgets all the sweet memories of his therapeutic liaison with the fallen woman.

Purab Aur Paschim

1970

Cast Manoj Kumar, Saira Banu, Bharathi, Kamini Kaushal, Madan Puri, Shammi, Prem Chopra
Director Manoj Kumar
Music Kalyanji, Anandji
Lyrics Indivar, Santosh Anand, Prem Dhawan

Writer-director Manoj Kumar's back-to-the-roots saga featured him as the archetypal patriot Bharat who faces the 'polluting' aspects of western culture in England, when the bleached-blonde Indian (Saira Banu) enters his holier-than-thou life. Famous mainly for Banu's scandalous short-skirted cigarette-smoking persona, *Purab Aur Paschim* threw forward an interesting debate on the downside of western culture and the devaluation of Indianess for a dream-chasing materialism. The message of nationalism ends with Banu and her parents returning to their roots.

TIMELINE: FILMS AND LANDMARK EVENTS

1970	**1970**	**1970**	1970	1971
Mera Gaon Mera Desh	**Purab Aur Paschim** (See p. 42)	**Safar** (See p. 43)	Sawan Bhadon	Aashas Ka Ek Din

1947

Indian cinema's most influential icon Lata Mangeshkar, sings her first Hindi song *Pa lagoon kar jori* in the film *Aap Ki Sewa Mein*.

Cast Ashok Kumar, Rajesh Khanna, Sharmila Tagore, Feroz Khan
Director Asit Sen
Music Kalyanji, Anandji
Lyrics Indivar

One of the string of films that Rajesh Khanna did playing on his image of the tragic dying hero. In *Safar* he's cast as an artist who sacrifices his love when he gets to know he is terminally ill. Feroz Khan as the suspicious and possessive husband got a rare chance to make an impact in a romantic film. Both Khanna and Tagore built on their images from their earlier hits *Aradhana* and *Amar Prem* as eternal romanticists. Though this film was far less successful than the other two it is noteworthy for its mature view of the man-woman relationship. There are no safe options in the plot. The tangled love triangle is resolved with the heroine bereft of the companionship of both men. Khanna's tragic persona was heightened by Kishore Kumar's pensive songs *Jeevan se bhari teri aankhen* and *Zindagi ka safar*.

Khilona (1970) was Shatrughan Sinha's first major foray into bad-man's territory. Sinha got the role on Mumtaz's recommendation. In a role turned down by Sharmila Tagore, Mumtaz brought both sauciness and sublimity. Producer Prasad's lucky mascot Jeetendra put in a 'friendly' appearance as the good-hearted lover-boy.

1971	1971	1971	**1971**	**1971**
Adhikar	Aisa Bhi Hota Hai	Albela	**Amar Prem** (See p. 44)	**Anand** (See p. 44)

1947

Legendary actor K.L. Saigal, who acted in P.C. Barua's *Devdas* (1935) passes away.

Anand
1971

Cast Rajesh Khanna, Sumita Sanyal, Ramesh Deo,
Seema Deo, Johnny Walker, Amitabh Bachchan
Director Hrishikesh Mukherjee
Music Salil Chowdhury
Lyrics Gulzar

This ravishing reiteration of Rajesh Khanna's indomitable superstardom also laid down the foundation stone of the Bachchan empire. If Khanna played the fading light of sunshine, Bachchan played the brooding and intense cloud. If one was the ever-grinning heart stealer the other was the ever-grim cynic, horrified by the malpractices in his medical profession, determined to save his dying friend from the clutches of cancer. Essentially a melodramatic tear-jerker, director Hrishikesh Mukherjee turned the drama of mortality into an immortal affirmation of life.

Amar Prem
1971

Cast Rajesh Khanna, Sharmila Tagore, Master Bobby
Vinod Mehra, Bindu, Sujit Kumar
Director Shakti Samanta
Music R.D. Burman
Lyrics Anand Bakshi

Two years after his historic *Aradhana,* Shakti Samanta assembled the same team for an artistic encore. *Amar Prem* is the unique story of a bonding beyond blood that grows among 3 social outcasts. a lonely neglected husband (Rajesh Khanna), a golden-hearted prostitute (Sharmila Tagore) and a sensitive little boy (Master Bobby) ill-treated by his stepmother (Bindu). Strong in her frailties, Sharmila Tagore's Pushpa is redolent of the image of the Indian woman as the Mother Godess: nurturing and all-giving in her selflessness. Unarguably one of R.D. Burman's most flawless scores to complement a film that has no blind spots, only the luminous light of a life well lived.

TIMELINE: FILMS AND LANDMARK EVENTS

1971	**1971**	1971	1971	1971
Andaz	**Anubhav**	Balidaan	Budda Mil Gaya	Caravan
(See p. 45)	(See p. 46)			

1947

Vijay Bhatt's *Ram Rajya,* A.R. Kardar's *Shah Jahan* and V. Shantaram's *Dr Kotnis Ki Amar Kahani* are shown at the Canadian National Exhibition in Toronto.

Cast Shammi Kapoor, Hema Malini, Simi Garewal, Rajesh Khanna
Director Ramesh Sippy
Music Shankar, Jaikishan
Lyrics Hasrat Jaipuri

Ramesh Sippy's directorial debut, this handsomely mounted romantic drama 'dared' to bring together a widow (Hema Malini) and a widower (Shammi Kapoor). The relationship is shown to grow through their respective children. The plot makes room for two lengthy flashbacks of the protagonists with their respective spouses. Shammi Kapoor's past-recall with his dead wife (Simi Garewal) is overshadowed by Hema's rabble-rousing rapport with Rajesh Khanna. Khanna's guest appearance at the peak of his superstardom, singing the super-hit *Zindagi ek safar hai suhana* only to die early in the plot, became the benchmark for all star guest appearances. Besides the film's understated formulism and Khanna's winsome guest appearance the film is memorable for attempting the theme of widow remarriage.

Rajesh Khanna's part in *Anand* (1971) was first offered by director Hrishikesh Mukherjee to Kishore Kumar, Shashi Kapoor and even Raj Kapoor! In fact the film was inspired by the director's close friendship with Raj Kapoor and the fear of losing a precious friend. Rajesh Khanna walked away with the Filmfare's best-actor award for his delicate delineation of a dying man's life-enforcing ebullience.

1971	1971	1971	1971	1971
Do Boond Pani	Do Rahen	Dost Aur Dushman	Duniya Kya Jane	Ek Adhuri Kahani

1948

Dev Anand becomes the first matinee idol with *Ziddi*, and remains at the top for more than thirty years.

Anubhav

1971

Cast Sanjeev Kumar, Tanuja, Dinesh Thakur, A.K. Hangal
Director Basu Bhattacharya
Music Kanu Roy
Lyrics Gulzar

In an era when Eastmancolour had invaded Hindi cinema to a monopolistic extent, the enterprising Basu Bhattacharya dared to venture

into the black-and-white world to portray the barren marriage of Meeta (Tanuja) to Amar (Sanjeev Kumar). On the brink of disintegration, their bleak togetherness gets a further jolt when Amar's colleague and Meeta's ex-boyfriend (Dinesh Thakur) barges into their lives. The friction caused by a third person in the marriage is delineated with brush-strokes of quiet intensity.

Guddi

1971

Cast Dharmendra, Jaya Bhaduri, Samit Bhanja, A.K. Hangal, Utpal Dutt
Director Hrishikesh Mukherjee
Music Vasant Desai   **Lyrics** Gulzar

In what is arguably the most appealing debut performance ever, Jaya Bhaduri stole millions of hearts as the chirpy schoolgirl who has a major crush on film star Dharmendra. The quirky comic drama delineates Guddi's growth from a star-stuck fan to a responsible and sensible woman who knows the difference between the illusion of celluloid and the reality outside. While interpreting celluloid dreams for the audience, director Hrishikesh Mukherjee invited a gallery of stars to make guest appearances. There are many illuminating illustrations of the star-fan bonding, like *Guddi* enraptured in the darkness of a theatre watching her idol Dharmendra in Hrishikesh Mukherjee's *Anupama*, or Guddi fantasizing about Dharmendra singing *Mujhe jeevan ki dor se bandh liya hai* (the song that Dev Anand and Sadhana lip-synced in Hrishikesh Mukherjee's *Asli Naqli*).

▶

TIMELINE: FILMS AND LANDMARK EVENTS

1971	1971	1971	**1971**	1971
Ek Paheli	Elaan	Gambler	**Guddi** (See p. 46)	Haathi Mere Saathi

1948

S.S. Vasan's lavish costume drama *Chandralekha* becomes the first Madras-produced success in Hindi cinema.

Cast Raj Kapoor, Manoj Kumar, Dharmendra, Rajendra Kumar, Dara Singh, Simi Garewal, Ksiena Rabiankina, Padmini, Rishi Kapoor

Director Raj Kapoor

Music Shankar, Jaikishan

Lyrics Shailendra, Hasrat Jaipuri, Neeraj, Prem Dhawan

A sprawling 4-hour epic tells the biographical story of a circus clown Raju (Raj Kapoor) who faces heartbreak three times over. In the first and by far the most relaxed chapter adolescent Raju (played by Raj Kapoor's son Rishi Kapoor) attains sexual awakening through his teacher (Simi Garewal) who is engaged to marry Manoj Kumar. In the second chapter Raju (Raj Kapoor) is part of his father's profession as a clown in the circus. He has a cute liaison with a stunning trapeze artiste (Ksiena Rabiankina) that ends in disaster. In the third most voluptuous chapter inspired by Charlie Chaplin's *Limelight,* Kapoor is mentor to an ambitious wannabe star (Padmini) who quickly latches on to a superstar (Rajendra Kumar) and deserts poor Raju. The heartbreaks culminate in the marvellous on-stage display of showmanship. Kapoor's reputation as the consummate showman is amply justified by the use of stars, colour, music, drama and romance.

Though without a background in Bollywood, Jaya Bhaduri carved a niche for herself there within no time. Little did she know that her endearing debut in *Guddi* (1971) would herald an era of stardom for her and catapult her to the status of being the 'First Lady of Bollywood' —Mrs Bachchan!

1971	**1971**	**1971**	1971	**1971**
Kal Aaj Aur Kal	**Mera Naam Joker** (See p. 47)	**Mere Apne** (See p. 48)	Naya Zamana	**Pakeezah** (See p. 48)

1948

Prolific filmmaker and actor Raj Kapoor sets up R.K. Studios.

Mere Apne

1971

Cast Meena Kumari, Vinod Khanna, Shatrughan
 Sinha, Danny Denzongpa, Paintal
Director Gulzar
Music Salil Chowdhury
Lyrics Gulzar

For his directorial debut, Gulzar adapted Tapan Sinha's Bengali hit *Apanjan*. Chronicling the compelling gang war between two student groups, *Mere Apne* pre-empted the youthful violence and unrest of Ram Gopal Varma's directorial debut *Shiva* as well as Mani Ratnam's *Yuva*. Shatrughan Sinha and Vinod Khanna seethe in a realistic rage as rival student leaders. Meena Kumari in her last screen appearance holds the plot and characters together. Playing a village woman who brings the rivals together through her gentle compassion Meena Kumari created a character that was soft and subtle.

Pakeezah

1971

Cast Meena Kumari, Ashok Kumar, Raj Kumar, Veena,
 Nadira
Director Kamal Amrohi
Music Ghulam Mohamed Naushad
Lyrics Kaifi Azmi, Majrooh Sultanpuri, Kaif Bhopali

Released days before the untimely death of its leading lady, *Pakeezah* rode to immortality on the wings of Meena Kumari's image of tragic grandeur. She was cast by her estranged husband as the archetypal *tawaif*, the courtesan who remains pure and virtuous through a series of highly romantic adventures that bring her closer to happiness. Meena Kumari dazzled in reposeful resplendence as a prostitute, penning poems of pain and romance in an environment of decadence. Amrohi takes her on a journey in search of love. ▶ When a romantic stranger (Raj Kumar) sees the courtesan's feet in a train compartment he falls in love with the woman and makes the classic observation, 'Don't let your feet touch the ground. They'll get soiled.' The film finally builds to a karmic spiral around Meena Kumari's tragic persona.

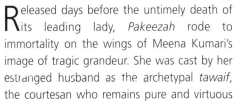

TIMELINE: FILMS AND LANDMARK EVENTS

1971	1971	**1971**	1972	1972
Parwana	Piya Ka Ghar	**Reshma Aur Shera** (See p. 49)	Apna Desh	Bawarchi

1949

The Films Division is set up in Bombay.

Reshma Aur Shera

1971   **DRAMA** 49

Cast Sunil Dutt, Waheeda Rehman, Amitabh Bachchan, Raakhee Gulzar
Director Sunil Dutt
Music Jaidev
Lyrics Balkavi Bairagi, Neeraj

A legendary love tale in the tradition of *Heer-Ranjha* and *Romeo & Juliet,* the lovers of this violent tale are located in the deserts of Rajasthan. The lush location provides director Dutt with ample scope to shoot the violence of uncontrollable passions and familial feuds in vivid glory. The narrative takes Reshma (Waheeda Rehman) and Shera (Sunil Dutt) through a series of tumultuous encounters. One of them involves a lengthy narrative song *Tu chanda main chandni* sung with the undulating lucidity of the sand dunes by Lata Mangeshkar, where the lovers meet, spend time together and part in operatic motions. Dutt uses non-cinematic modes to express the grief, rage and passion of an unreasonably exacerbated climate. Both the principal players are credible, though their thunder is often stolen by bit-players Bachchan (playing the hero's sibling) and Raakhee.

Although Meena Kumari was too ill to perform all the intricate *mujra* dances in *Pakeezah* (1971) herself, this is Meena Kumari's most memorable role. The danseuse-actress Padma Khanna performed the climactic song posing as Meena Kumari with a veil hiding her face.

1972	1972	1972	1972	**1972**
Beimaan	Bijlee	Bombay to Goa	Ek Hasina Do Diwane	**Hare Rama Hare Krishna** (See p. 50)

1949

Countrywide closure of cinemas in protest against the Government's taxation policy.

Hare Rama Hare Krishna 1972

Cast Dev Anand, Mumtaz, Zeenat Aman
Director Dev Anand
Music R.D. Burman
Lyrics Anand Bakshi

Dev Anand's most successful film as a director, the novel location (Kathmandu) and the hard-hitting theme (a maladjusted girl's tryst with drug trafficking and other intriguing tangles in the cloistered bylanes of Kathmandu) ensured a sizeable audience interest—the sensational depiction of the drugged hippy cult, chart-busting songs like *Dum maro dum* and *I love you*, and Zeenat Aman in her post-debut appearance, striking the right trendy and rebellious notes as the hero's drugged derelict sister Janice thumbing her nose at convention.

Koshish 1972

Cast Sanjeev Kumar, Jaya Bhaduri, Om Shivpuri, Asrani
Director Gulzar
Music Madan Mohan
Lyrics Gulzar

Gulzar's post-debut directorial creation was a marvel of silent splendour. Boldly departing from convention, it depicts the life and struggle of a deaf-and-mute couple to live in an uncaring world with dignity and joy. Both Sanjeev Kumar and Jaya Bhaduri (the latter replaced Moushumi Chatterjee at the eleventh hour) turn in superlative-defining performances. Though it was Kumar who walked away with the National Award, most admirers of the actress and this mutely moving drama believe Bhaduri was every bit as credible. Without a word exchanged, the lead pair expresses a universe of emotions.

TIMELINE: FILMS AND LANDMARK EVENTS

1972	1972	**1972**	1972	**1972**
Hawas	Izzat	**Koshish** (See p. 50)	Mere Jeevan Saathi	**Parichay** (See p. 51)

1949

Lata Mangeshkar changes the face of playback singing with a multitude of chartbusters in the films *Bazar*, *Barsat*, *Badi Bahen*, *Andaz*, *Dulari*, *Lahore* and *Mahal*.

Parichay

Cast Jeetendra, Jaya Bhaduri, Pran, Sanjeev Kumar
Director Gulzar
Music R.D. Burman
Lyrics Gulzar

Parichay is based on a Bengali short story. It is the story of the estranged grandchildren of Rai Sahib (Pran) who had once disowned his singer-son (Sanjeev Kumar). Now the children are back to create a ruckus in the well-ordered life of grandpa. Enter the teacher Jeetendra, with moustache and spectacles in place, giving the actor a serious image. The subtle, almost unstated romance between the teacher and his eldest student (Jaya Bhaduri) is fuelled by the antics of the bratty kids. The film contained an outstanding music score by Burman. The songs included Kishore Kumar's *Musafir hoon yaaron* (filmed as the teacher travels down to his new students' destination) and the National Award-winning *Beeti na beetaayi raina*, rendered hauntingly by Lata Mangeshkar and Bhupinder and filmed on 'daughter' Jaya and 'father' Sanjeev Kumar.

Besides launching Zeenat Aman as a major star of the 1970s *Hare Rama Hare Krishna* (1972) also consolidated R.D. Burman's position as one of the foremost music composers of the pre-electronic era with a sound that was fresh, bracing and young.

1972	1972	**1973**	**1973**	**1973**
Seeta Aur Geeta	Shor	**Abhimaan**	**Ankur**	**Avishkar**
		(See p. 52)	(See p. 144)	(See p. 114)

1951

The Central Board of Film Censors is formed. Noted filmmaker P.C. Barua, famous for his film *Devdas* (1935), starring K.L Saigal and Jamuna.

Abhimaan 1973

Cast Amitabh Bachchan, Jaya Bhaduri, Bindu, Asrani, Durga Khote
Director Hrishikesh Mukherjee
Music S.D. Burman
Lyrics Majrooh Sultanpuri

That recurrent love-defining moment featuring the hero's first glimpse of the heroine takes place in *Abhimaan* when Amitabh Bachchan, playing a popular singer, sees the rustic Jaya Bhaduri singing *Nadiya kinare* at the riverbank. Love, belonging, marriage, envy and atonement form the core of *Abhimaan*—Mukherjee explored the male ego and how it smothers a wife's indomitable talent. From her introductory song to *Piya bina piya bina* (where the wife sings on stage of her husband's growing intolerance) to the climactic *Tere mere milan ki yeh raina* (the reunion of the repentant husband with his shell-shocked wife) Lata Mangeshkar virtually transported this film to a classic status. Jaya closely studied Lata Mangeshkar's working in the recording studio before tackling the role.

Daag 1973

Cast Rajesh Khanna, Sharmila Tagore, Raakhee, Prem Chopra
Director Yash Chopra
Music Laxmikant, Pyarelal
Lyrics Sahir Ludhianvi

Daag is a triangular melodrama based on the pulp bestseller by the Hindi novelist Gulshan Nanda. It is the dizzying story of a man (Rajesh Khanna) presumed to be dead by his pregnant wife (Sharmila Tagore). Many years later, he surfaces in another town with another identity as the husband of the woman, Raakhee, who has given shelter to the missing man's wife and child. The second-half of the film is a beguiling and ambiguous ode to bigamy with the man, now appointed mayor of the scenic town where the triangle plays itself out, shuttles tantalizingly between the two women seeking to find a common ground between his past and present.

TIMELINE: FILMS AND LANDMARK EVENTS

1973	1973	1973	1973	1973
Bobby	**Daag**	Dhund	**Garam Hawa**	Gehri Chaal
(See p. 126)	(See p. 52)		(See p. 53)	

1952

Aan and *Jhansi ki Rani* are made in colour.

Garam Hawa

1973

Cast Balraj Sahni, Geeta Siddharth, Shaukat Azmi, Farooq Shaikh
Director M.S. Sathyu
Music Bahadur Khan
Lyrics Kaifi Azmi

A poignant and authentic depiction of the trauma following the partition of India and Pakistan, and the dispossession of the Indian Muslims that followed, as they careened between their old home and new land. *Garam Hawa* chronicles the geo-political and moral conflict of Salim Mirza (Balraj Sahni) who loses family, property and self-regard in the transition. He chooses to stay back in India with his children, certain that India has a safe and productive future for the minority communities. Sathyu's directorial debut was a strong political commentary as well as an utterly moving drama of displacement played out against the bustling backdrop of Agra.

Balraj Sahni's last performance *Garam Hawa* (1973) before his death is considered by many film buffs to be the single most authentic portrayal of upheaval and redemption in Indian cinema.

1973	1973	1973	1973	1973
Namak Haram	**Phagun**	**Rajnigandha**	Saudagar	Yaadon Ki Baraat
(See p. 53)	(See p. 54)	(See p. 144)		

1952

The First International Film Festival held in India, and travels to Bombay, Calcutta, Delhi and Madras.

Namak Haram 1973

Cast Rajesh Khanna, Amitabh Bachchan, Rekha, Simi Garewal
Director Hrishikesh Mukherjee
Music R.D. Burman
Lyrics Anand Bakshi

Arguably the most powerful drama in Mukherjee's commodious oeuvre, *Namak Haram* looks at the question of class divide within the purview of the troubled relationship between the capitalist-industrialist Amitabh Bachchan and his proletariat friend Rajesh Khanna. Their stormy relationship gives the plot a narrative energy that builds up to a tragic climax. Memorable for its powerful theme, *Namak Haram* featured Bachchan at his implosive best fuming against a class distinction that he didn't create.

Phagun 1973

Cast Waheeda Rehman, Dharmendra, Jaya Bhaduri, Vijay Arora
Director Rajinder Singh Bedi
Music S.D. Burman
Lyrics Majrooh Sultanpuri

Rajinder Singh Bedi whose directorial debut *Dastak* signalled a psychologically dense treatment of the man-woman relationship went deeper into the theme in *Phagun*. In one of her last films as a leading lady Waheeda Rehman played the complex part of a traumatized wife. Deserted by her husband (Dharmendra) she channels her affections into supervising the life of her daughter (Jaya Bhaduri) whose marriage further complicates familial issues. The sequence where the mother imagines herself with her head on her son-in-law's shoulders raised many eyebrows. This was one of the rare Indian films to focus on a mother-daughter bonding. Rehman and Bhaduri warmly played the two central parts. The film systematically wiped out Rehman's career as a romantic leading lady. Henceforth she was only offered mothers' parts.

TIMELINE: FILMS AND LANDMARK EVENTS

1973	**1974**	1974	1974	1974
Zanjeer	**Aap Ki Kasam** (See p. 55)	Benaam	Bidaai	Haath Ki Safayi

1952

The Parliament passes the Cinematograph Act, replacing the Act of 1918.

Aap Ki Kasam

1974 **DRAMA** 55

Cast Rajesh Khanna, Mumtaz, Sanjeev Kumar
Director J. Om Prakash
Music R.D. Burman
Lyrics Anand Bakshi

Though the first-half of this marital drama is devoted entirely to romantic preoccupations, *Aap Ki Kasam* builds up into a startling second-half where Mumtaz, in one of her final roles as a leading lady, plays the wife of a suspicious husband who decides to walk out on her home and husband. The last lap of the slightly luminous projection of a splintered relationship shows the repentant hero trying to redeem his troubled conscience. The plot's emotional content holds together, thanks to the main performances by Rajesh Khanna (in one of his last films as a successful leading man), Mumtaz and Sanjeev Kumar (playing the couple's innocuous neighbour who becomes a bone of contention). Director J. Om Prakash who made other socially relevant films like *Asha, Apnapan* and *Aadmi Khilona Hai*, preferred Laxmikant-Pyarelal to score music for his films. R.D. Burman's music is a highlight of *Aap Ki Kasam*. Songs like *Jai jai shiv shankar* and *Karvaten badalte rahen* play up the crackling chemistry between the leading pair.

One of Jaya Bhaduri's personal favourites, she has expressed the desire to remake *Phagun* (1973) casting herself as the mother and Kajol as the daughter.

1974	1974	**1974**	1974	**1974**
Heera Panna	Kasauti	**Kora Kaagaz** (See p. 56)	Majboor	**Roti Kapda Aur Makan** (See p. 56)

1953

Two years after meeting at the music recording for songs for the film *Baazi* (1951), director Guru Dutt and playback singer Geeta Roy get married. Geeta Dutt continues to do playback singing for Guru Dutt's films despite a somewhat tumultuous marriage.

Kora Kaagaz 1974

Cast Jaya Bhaduri, Vijay Anand, Achala Sachdev,
A.K. Hangal, Nazneen
Director Anil Ganguly
Music Kalyanji, Anandji
Lyrics M.G. Hashmat

A remake of Ajoy Kar's 1963 successful Bengali marital drama *Saat Paake Bandha* featured Jaya Bhaduri and Vijay Anand as a husband and wife torn apart by the arrogant interference of the wife's mother (Achala Sachdev). There are some extremely intense moments of friction between the couple, for example the celebrated sequence where in a fit of rage, the wife tears her husband's kurta. Kishore Kumar's Filmfare Award-winning title song added a poignant note to this minor but moving drama.

Roti Kapda Aur Makan 1974

Cast Manoj Kumar, Zeenat Aman, Amitabh Bachchan,
Shashi Kapoor, Moushumi Chatterjee, Premnath
Director Manoj Kumar
Music Laxmikant, Pyarelal
Lyrics Santosh Anand, Verma Malik

The huge star-cast and Manoj Kumar's formidable reputation as the harbinger of formulistic patriotism ensured a sizeable audience for this rather-engrossing look at economic recession joblessness and moral decline in the India of the 1970s. Cast as Bharat, Manoj Kumar takes potshots at the cult of consumerism through his girlfriend Zeenat Aman's ambiguous morality. She dumps Kumar to marry the moneyed tycoon Shashi Kapoor. A charismatic cast including Moushumi Chatterjee as a rape victim (her controversial rape sequence was shot in a flurry of flour mounds) and Amitabh Bachchan as the cynical sibling to the hero, plus a terrific music score added to the film's mass appeal.

TIMELINE: FILMS AND LANDMARK EVENTS

1975	1975	1975	1975	1975
Aandhi	**Chotisi Baat**	**Chupke Chupke**	**Deewaar**	Dharmatma
(See p. 57)	(See p. 100)	(See p. 101)	(See p. 58)	

1953

India's first technicolour film *Jhansi Ki Rani* by Sohrab Modi is released. He had technicians flown in from Hollywood, and the production cost 9 million Indian rupees.

Aandhi

Cast Suchitra Sen, Sanjeev Kumar, Om Prakash, A. K. Hangal, Rehman

Director Gulzar

Music R. D. Burman

Lyrics Gulzar

Starting with the lady politician's arrival in a dusty town for an election campaign, *Aandhi* trails Arati Devi (Suchitra Sen) into her past life where we see her marriage falling apart due to her father's (Rehman) political aspirations. In the present, the lady finds herself facing her long-estranged husband (Sanjeev Kumar). Besides the obvious political allusions, the narrative raises a very critical question. Does a celebrity, particularly a woman and that too a national leader, have the right to a private life, and how justified is the media in prying into famous lives? These questions assume a hankering nostalgia as the now-reunited couple exchange old memories and fresh melodies amidst symbolical archeological ruins. Suchitra Sen, coaxed into a very rare and final appearance in a Hindi film, furnishes the protagonist's role with a precious tragedy.

Gulzar's *Aandhi* (1975) derives its main thematic thrust from the life of the amazing Indira Gandhi. The basic plot about a woman (played by Suchitra Sen) whose political aspirations ruin her personal life is loosely based on real-life incidents. *Aandhi* was released during Mrs Gandhi's infamous state of Emergency in the country. There were instant protests about the real-life parallels.

1975	1975	**1975**	**1975**	**1975**
Faraar	Jai Santoshi Maa	**Julie**	**Khushboo**	**Mili**
		(See p. 126)	(See p. 58)	(See p. 59)

(See p. 126)   (See p. 58)   (See p. 59)

1954

Bimal Roy's *Do Bigha Zameen* (1953) gets special mention at the Cannes Film Festival.

Deewaar

1975

Cast Amitabh Bachchan, Shashi Kapoor, Neetu Singh, Parveen Babi, Nirupa Roy

Director Yash Chopra

Music R.D. Burman

Lyrics Sahir Ludhianvi

*D*eewaar reiterated the patent themes of commercial Hindi cinema—the mother as the supreme arbitrator and brothers at loggerheads. Salim-Javed's script gave a startling twist to traditional formulas. Vijay (Bachchan) and the law-abiding Mama's boy Ravi (Kapoor). *Deewaar* is a story of human relationships with the mother figure (Nirupa Roy) standing tall over the moralistic machinations of the two brothers.

◄

Khushboo

1975

Cast Jeetendra, Hema Malini, Farida Jalal, Durga Khote, Sharmila Tagore

Director Gulzar

Music R.D. Burman

Lyrics Gulzar

*T*he poet-filmmaker Gulzar's fifth feature film ferreted out a novel by Bengali litterateur Saratchandra Chatterjee dealing with the issue of child marriage. Hema Malini and Jeetendra played relatively deglamourized rustic characters grappling with convention, through a series of strange circumstances. The performances, including Sharmila Tagore playing a derelict woman whom Jeetendra 'rescues' and marries, though 'filmy', are unstrained. R.D. Burman's ethereal music score makes *Khushboo* emanate the fragrance of nostalgia and poetry.

TIMELINE: FILMS AND LANDMARK EVENTS

1975	1976	**1976**	1976	1976
Sholay (See p. 60)	Hera Pheri	**Kabhi Kabhie** (See p. 127)	Kalicharan	Manthan

1954

The Indian Film Festival is held in the (former) Soviet Union.

Mili

Cast Ashok Kumar, Amitabh Bachchan, Jaya Bhaduri, Usha Kiron
Director Hrishikesh Mukherjee
Music S.D. Burman
Lyrics Yogesh

Deewaar (1975) was the first mainstream film to legitimize the underworld. The film also features Amitabh Bachchan in his only bare-chested bed sequence ever! Nirupa Roy features in an award-winning role that was first offered to Vyjanthimala.

Extending the director's pet theme of the do-gooder's cruel end through death in *Anand*, Hrishikesh Mukherjee turned Rajesh Khanna's character from the earlier film into the giggly and lovable Mili (Jaya Bhaduri). After winning everyone's hearts Mili finally extends her bonhomie to the brooding alcoholic Bachchan. Their togetherness seems short-lived when Mili is diagnosed with cancer. Unlike *Anand*, this films ends on a note of hope with Bachchan's character insisting on marrying the ill girl and taking her abroad for treatment. *Mili* is memorable for the lead pair's intense performance and for S.D. Burman's music, composed for the film while he was on his deathbed. This was the super-successful Bhaduri's final film before her marriage. She made a comeback 6 years later in Yash Chopra's *Silsila*.

1976	1977	1977	**1977**	1977
Mausam (See p. 60)	Adalat	Alaap	**Amar Akbar Anthony** (See p. 61)	Anurodh

1956

R.K. Films' *Jagte Raho* wins the Grand Prix at the Karlovy Vary Film Festival.

Sholay   1975

Cast Dharmendra, Hema Malini, Amitabh Bachchan,
Jaya Bhaduri, Sanjeev Kumar, Amjad Khan
Director Ramesh Sippy
Music R.D. Burman   **Lyrics** Anand Bakshi

India's most popular action film, *Sholay* tells the gripping epic story of two petty criminals Jai (Amitabh Bachchan) and Veeru (Dharmendra) and their efforts to seek revenge on behalf of a sullen landlord (Sanjeev Kumar) from a boorish and vicious dacoit. The film's writers Salim and Javed must be credited for giving Hindi cinema one of its most abiding villains. As played by the relatively untried actor Amjad Khan, Gabbar Singh and his casually hip lines acquired an instantly legendary status among Hindi movie-goers. Dharmendra and Bachchan smoulder on screen as antithetical friends. The rest of the cast provide the constantly alert and accelerated narrative with just the right nuances to make this the most virile masala film from Bollywood.

Mausam   1976

Cast Sharmila Tagore, Sanjeev Kumar
Director Gulzar
Music Madan Mohan
Lyrics Gulzar

Derived directly from Hindi author Kamleshwar's *Agami Ateet*, Mausam is an elegiac tale of shadows and whispers told in bright flashbacks. Sanjeev Kumar plays a man confronted by his past when the daughter (Sharmila Tagore) of the woman he had loved and left comes unexpectedly into his life. The white-collar patriarch's rather risqué encounters with his prostitute-daughter form the core of this unusual drama. Tagore dropped her trademark mannerisms to play the whore with passion. Madan Mohan's nostalgic music score includes the Bhupinder-rendered ghazal *Dil dhoondta hai* and Asha Bhosle's comic seduction song *Mere ishq mein lakhon latke,* where the hooker unknowingly tries to hook her own father!

TIMELINE: FILMS AND LANDMARK EVENTS

1977	1977	**1977**	1977	1977
Bhumika (See p. 145)	Dharam Veer	**Dulhan Wohi Jo Piya Man Bhaye** (See p. 102)	Hum Kissise Kum Nahin	Inkaar

1956

Indian Talkies celebrates its Silver Jubilee in Bombay. The first Indian talkie (film with sound), *Alam Ara*, was released in 1931.

Amar Akbar Anthony　　　1977

Cast Amitabh Bachchan, Vinod Khanna, Rishi Kapoor, Parveen Babi,
　　Shabana Azmi, Neetu Singh, Pran, Nirupa Roy
Director Manmohan Desai
Music Laxmikant, Pyarelal
Lyrics Anand Bakshi

Awalloping, kitschy blues-chaser from Manmohan Desai, *Amar Akbar Anthony* were played by Vinod Khanna, Rishi Kapoor and Amitabh Bachchan. The mind-boggling twists and turns take the three estranged 'long-lost' brothers through a maelstrom of adventures, romance, comedy and drama. Desai who went on to become the most commercially successful filmmaker of the 1970s didn't consider this to be his favourite film. But the audiences disagreed. Over the years the film's message of religious secularism has seeped into the very essence of popular visual culture. Many sequences such as the one where the inebriated Anthony (Bachchan) talks with his mirror image have become a part of movie folklore. Though Rishi Kapoor as the happy-go-lucky qawwali singer steals much of the narrative's sunshine (and the hit Rafi qawwali *Parda hai parda*) it is Bachchan who carries the show to its blockbuster status.

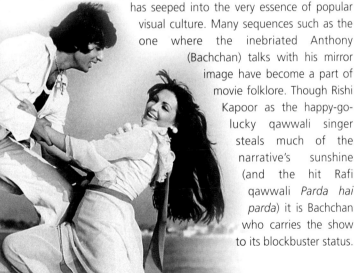

Sholay (1975) declared a dud on its release, became one of the greatest grossers of all times after its third week. Danny Denzongpa had declined the role of Gabbar Singh. Portions of this lengthy film were deleted initially and added later when the film became a hit. The Bachchan-Dharmendra combination crackled with the chemistry of male camaraderie. *Sholay* is one of the most emulated of Hindi films.

1977	1977	**1977**	**1977**	1977
Khoon Pasina	Kinara	**Kitaab** (See p. 62)	**Laila Majnu** (See p. 128)	Mandir Masjid

1957

Sunil Dutt and Nargis who both acted in *Mother India* (1957) marry.

Doosra Aadmi

1977

Cast Raakhee, Rishi Kapoor, Neetu Singh,
Shashi Kapoor
Director Ramesh Talwar
Music Rajesh Roshan
Lyrics Majrooh Sultanpuri

Long before it became fashionable for Bollywood to depict a relationship between a young man and an older woman, Ramesh Talwar directed this film about a high-strung woman (perfectly played by Raakhee) who falls for a much younger man (Rishi Kapoor). Though the plot sought a deliberate escape route to ensure that moralists and conservatives don't jump on the film (the woman sees a facial similarity between the young man and her dead lover, played by Rishi's uncle Shashi Kapoor) it nonetheless dared to venture into a forbidden area during a decade when the man-woman relationship was crawling out of its infancy in Hindi cinema. Talwar created an elegiac tone in the doomed romance and saw the unlikely romance to its logical, tragical, finale. Comic actor Deven Varma played Neetu Singh's uncle and even sang a folk song *Ab na aayenge sanwariya* in his own voice, plus a technically polished look gave *Doosra Aadmi* a feeling of enchantment.

Kitaab

1977

Cast Master Rajoo (Raju Shrestha), Uttam Kumar,
Vidya Sinha
Director Gulzar
Music R.D. Burman
Lyrics Gulzar

Kitaab is a sweet story about a little boy's adventures away from his home, and his journey into a growing awareness of the world around him. Cannily crafted as an onward pilgrimage, Gulzar's film focussed on the young protagonist, to the extent that the grownup actors (including Bengali matinee idol Uttam Kumar and Vidya Sinha playing the child's parents) were relegated to the background. What emerged with compelling clarity was Gulzar's ability to fathom the complex world of the young.

TIMELINE: FILMS AND LANDMARK EVENTS

1977	1977	1977	1977	1978
Parvaish	Sharmilee	Shatranj Ke Khiladi	Yeh Hai Zindagi	Don

1957

Mehboob Khan's landmark film *Mother India* (1957) is the first Indian film to be nominated for an Oscar in the Best Foreign Film category.

Main Tulsi Tere Aangan Ki

Cast Nutan, Asha Parekh, Vijay Anand, Vinod Khanna, Somu Mukherjee

Director Raj Khosla

Music Laxmikant, Pyarelal

Lyrics Anand Bakshi

Made memorable by the first 20 minutes of playing time when the classic confrontation between the wife (Nutan) and the other woman (Asha Parekh) happens, this blockbuster from one of Hindi cinema's neglected directors, rapidly evolves into a good-son-bad-son potboiler with an abundance of kitsch. The later excesses do not take away from the beauty of the initial scenes where wife Nutan (in one of her last brilliant performances) first confronts her husband's (Vijay Anand) mistress Asha Parekh (wonderfully poised) and later adopts and brings up her husband's illegitimate son (Vinod Khanna). Laxmikant-Pyarelal came up with a memorable title song sung to ceaseless sublimity by Lata Mangeshkar. Khosla's films often resorted to bigamous drama, e.g. Rekha and Moushumi Chatterjee in *Daasi*, Waheeda Rehman and Sharmila Tagore in *Sunny*.

Just when it seemed that Asha Parekh was fated to do only light-hearted roles, she made a histrionic impact. Asha's talent came through in 1966, which saw her star in four successful films: *Teesri Manzil, Love in Tokyo, Aaye Din Bahaar Ke* and *Do Badan*. In 1970 she was awarded the Best Actress Award for her role as the widow with a secret in *Kati Patang*.

1978	1978	**1978**	**1978**	**1978**
Junoon (See p. 136)	Kasme Vaade	**Main Tulsi Tere Aangan Ki** (See p 63)	**Muqaddar Ka Sikandar** (See p. 64)	**Nishant** (See p. 146)

1958

The Indian Copyright Act comes into force.

Muqaddar Ka Sikandar 1978

Cast Amitabh Bachchan, Raakhee, Rekha,
   Vinod Khanna, Amjad Khan
Director Prakash Mehra
Music Kalyanji, Anandji
Lyrics Anjaan

A gravity-defying 5-angled romantic puzzle. By the time the quintet of characters clear their confusions, the fast-paced plot has gone through a series of partner-swapping rituals. Bachchan's role is essentially a variation on the *Devdas* prototype. The warm voluptuary of the *tawaif*, played by Rekha, counterpoises his doomed love for the unattainable Raakhee. One of the most successful products of the Mehra-Bachchan collaboration, *Muqaddar Ka Sikandar* acquired an enduring status.

Albert Pinto Ko Gussa Kyon Aata Hai 1980

Cast Naseeruddin Shah, Shabana Azmi, Smita Patil
Director Saeed Mirza
Music Manas Mukherjee, Bhaskar Chandavarkar
Lyrics Madhosh Bilgrami, Hriday Lani

A lbert Pinto Ko Gussa Kyon Aata Hai remains, to this day, director Saeed Mirza's most fiercely indignant portrayal of the rages of minorityism. In *Albert Pinto...*Mirza went for a compelling bird's-eye view of the problems that plague the Christian community. Mirza's unsentimental approach to the theme of segregation was punctuated by some detached moments of poignancy. Smita Patil playing the hero's physically challenged sister, gave a new dimension to the dignity of the working woman. At the film's end we no longer need to ask why Albert Pinto gets angry; we know.

TIMELINE: FILMS AND LANDMARK EVENTS

1978	1978	1979	1979	**1979**
Pati Patni Aur Woh (See p. 102)	Trishul	Atmaram	Bhayanak	**Ek Bar Phir** (See p. 146)

1958

V. Shantaram's *Do Aankhen Bara Haath* wins the President's Gold Medal, a Silver Bear at Berlin and the Samuel Goldwyn Award for Best Foreign Film

Karz

Cast Rishi Kapoor, Tina Munim, Simi Garewal, Raj Kiran, Durga Khote,
Premnath, Pran

Director Subhash Ghai

Music Laxmikant, Pyarelal

Lyrics Anand Bakshi

Subhash Ghai's adaptation of *The Reincarnation Of Peter Proud* was a major success, heralding the charismatic Rishi Kapoor as India's first rock star—an image that was further extended into Nasir Husain's musical films *Hum Kissise Kam Nahin* and *Zamanein Ko Dikhana Hai*. Dancing on a strobelit stage to the tune of Laxmikant-Pyarelal's *Om shanti om* and *Ek hasina thi* (which became the title of *Paisa yeh paisa*, Kapoor created a major impact among young movie-goers. For drama he played the reincarnation of a man (the Kapoor look-alike Raj Kiran) who takes revenge on the woman who killed him in his last life. Simi Garewal in one of her more memorable roles lent an icy sheath to her negative part. *Karz* held together as musical drama with lots of zestful choreography performed with lightning feet by Rishi Kapoor.

The hit film *Muqaddar Ka Sikandar* (1978) served to further solidify Amitabh Bachchan's cult status. His electrifying performance and Rekha's sophisticated act, replicating the sensuality of the courtesan Chandramukhi in *Devdas* (1935) made *Muqaddar...* an enduring classic.

1979	1979	1979	1979	1979
Golmaal (See p. 103)	Jurmaana	Kala Patthar	Magroor	Meera

(See p. 103)

1959

Bollywood's first film in Cinemascope, *Kaagaz Ke Phool,* is released.

Kalyug

1981

Cast Shashi Kapoor, Rekha, Raj Babbar, Victor
    Bannerjee, Anant Nag
Director Shyam Benegal
Music Vanraj Bhatia

A modern-day adaptation of the Hindu epic the Mahabharat, *Kalyug* was ambitious in scale and scope. It extracted specific characters, situations and incidents from the original epic and placed them within the cinematic format. The story holds together as an intense study of inter-personal tensions as transposed into a business domain. The performances were admirably 'epic'. As in Benegal's *Junoon* Shashi Kapoor (playing a contemporary version of Karna from the Mahabharat) produced this film.

Umrao Jaan

1981

Cast Rekha, Farooq Shaikh, Naseeruddin Shah,
    Raj Babbar, Shaukat Azmi
Director Muzaffar Ali
Music Khayyam   **Lyrics** Shahryar

Rekha's most well-known film features her as the real-life *tawaif* (courtesan) Umrao Jaan Adaa who undergoes a series of experiences replicating the capricious sexual escapades of Flaubert's Madame Bovary in a Mughal setting. Exquisitely styled, Rekha's central performance is immeasurably enhanced by Khayyam's songs and Asha Bhosle's vocals, yielding songs of love, life and other misadventures. Muzaffar Ali's most accomplished film, *Umrao Jaan* is suffused in the culture of Lucknow. The director brings alive the sights, sounds and scents of a culture and an ethos long-gone through exquisite painting-like shots capturing Rekha in regal splendour. After *Pakeezah,* this is the best known *tawaif's* tale.

TIMELINE: FILMS AND LANDMARK EVENTS				
1979	1979	1979	1979	1979
Mr Natwarlal	Naalayak	Noorie	Qurbani	Suhaag

1960

Kishore Kumar, actor as well as playback singer, weds the beautiful actress Madhubala, who immortalized the courtesan Anarkali in K. Asif's hit film, *Mughal-e-Azam,* released the same year.

Bemisaal

Cast Amitabh Bachchan, Raakhee, Vinod Mehra
Director Hrishikesh Mukherjee
Music R.D. Burman
Lyrics Anand Bakshi

*B*emisaal is one of Bachchan's best performances to date. The clenched jaw connoting a sense of bridled hopelessness and those pained eyes expressing infinite sorrow have never been used to more advantage. Playing an orphan who grows up to give up everything, including love, for his benefactor's son (Vinod Mehra), Bachchan shone like the sun at dawn. Besides being a brilliant treatise on loyalty, friendship and family ties, *Bemisal* also took time off to make comments on malpractices in the medical profession (a theme that Mukherjee had dwelled on earlier in *Anand*). The film has flashes of a believable bonding among Bachchan, Mehra and his screen-wife Raakhee. Especially notable is the chorus song *Yeh Kashmir hai* sung by all three protagonists during the Raakhee-Vinod Mehra honeymoon. There's a sense of intimate rapture in the way the three-way relationship functions in the script.

Beginning with *Anand* in 1970, Amitabh Bachchan collaborated with one of his favourite directors, Hrishikesh Mukherjee in *Abhimaan* (1973), *Namak Haram* (1973), *Mili* (1973) and *Chupke* (1975) *Chupke*. *Bemisaal* (1982) was their last team effort.

1979	**1980**	**1980**	1980	1980
The Great Gambler	**Aakrosh** (See p. 147)	**Albert Pinto Ko Gussa Kyon Aata Hai** (Seep. 64)	Do Aur Do Paanch	Insaaf Ka Taraazu

1960

The Film Finance Corporation, later to become National Film Development Corporation (NFDC) is founded.

Namkeen

1982

Cast Sanjeev Kumar, Waheeda Rehman,
Sharmila Tagore, Shabana Azmi, Kiran Vairele
Director Gulzar
Music R.D. Burman
Lyrics Gulzar

The poetic Gulzar's most nostalgic film, *Namkeen* is rendered unforgettable by its gallery of female performers. Waheeda Rehman plays the senile mother to three daughters, Tagore, Azmi and Vairele. Abandoned by the man of the house they live in a state of suspended desolation in a hill station. The arrival of a truck driver Sanjeev Kumar creates an unforeseen excitement and complications in the women's lives. The actresses confer a captivating light on this Ingmar Bergmanesque study of women and their substance. Shabana as the mute Mithu roams the stunning landscape to the sound of Asha Bhosle's evocative *Phir se aiyo badra bidesi*. Such magical moments occur repeatedly in this intimate study of human dereliction and redemption.

Prem Rog

1982

Cast Padmini Kolhapure, Rishi Kapoor, Nanda,
Shammi Kapoor, Tanuja, Sushma Seth
Director Raj Kapoor   **Music** Laxmikant, Pyarelal
Lyrics Santosh Anand, Amir Qazalbash, Pandit
Narendra Sharma

Raj Kapoor's most socially relevant film goes into the theme of widow remarriage. A pampered village girl (Kolhapure) goes from oblivious ecstasy to damning tragedy after her husband (Vijayendra Ghatge) dies hours after their wedding. In her most memorable screen appearance Kolhapure brought poignancy to sequences such as the ritualistic shearing of the ▶ widow's hair. Rishi Kapoor is commendably muted as her silent lover. Raj Kapoor blends a social message with his habitually voyeuristic approach to female beauty. Laxmikant-Pyarelal's hit music score includes Lata Mangeshkar's chartbuster *Yeh galiyan yeh chaubara* where Kolhapure sings and dances in celebration of her own marriage. The film's high-voltage treatment of a sensitive issue sparked off a sizable curiosity among audiences.

TIMELINE: FILMS AND LANDMARK EVENTS

1980	**1980**	1980	1981	1981
Karz	**Khubsoorat**	Shaan	Angoor	Barsaat Ki Ek Raat
(See p. 65)	(See p. 104)			

1960

The Film and Television Institute of India (FTII) is set up in Pune.

Saath Saath

Cast Farooq Shaikh, Deepti Naval
Director Raman Kumar
Music Kuldeep Singh
Lyrics Javed Akhtar

A film about the end of idealism, *Saath Saath* featured an invigorating new pair. As the newly married couple whose dreams of a perfect togetherness is stymied by the stench of corruption, Shaikh and Naval turned in fresh, natural performances. They went on to form a hit pair in several subsequent sub-standard films, thereby ironically illustrating this film's theme of the end of idealism. Television director Raman Kumar in his feature-film debut brought a bracing innovativeness to Hindi cinema. Songs like *Tumko dekha to yeh khayaal aaya* sung by Jagjit Singh extended the mood of authenticity. The film was flush with fresh faces, many of who went on to do a lot of television.

Padmini Kolhapure had her breakthrough in Bollywood at the tender age of 12 in Raj Kapoor's *Satyam Shivam Sundaram* (1979). Considering her age, Padmini was a phenomenon—she won two Filmfare awards for Best Supporting Actress in *Insaaf ka Taraazu* (1980) and Best Actress for *Prem Rog* (1982) when she was 13 and 15 years of age respectively!

1981	1981	1981	1981	1981
Chakra	**Chashme Buddoor**	**Ek Duuje Ke Liye**	**Kalyug**	Khoon Ka Khoon
(See p. 148)	(See p. 104)	(See p. 128)	(See p. 66)	

1960

K. Asif's *Mughal-e-Azam* is a huge success.

Shakti

1982

Cast Dilip Kumar, Raakhee, Amitabh Bachchan, Smita Patil
Director Ramesh Sippy
Music R.D. Burman   **Lyrics** Anand Bakshi

Super-successful scriptwriting duo Salim-Javed's finest effort and director Ramesh Sippy's most deftly packaged drama is in many ways superior to his historic *Sholay*. Dilip Kumar and Amitabh Bachchan as father and son, aligning on opposite sides of a nebulous line of morality, turned out extraordinarily fine-tuned performances. Indignance appears to be a perfect foil to the other performance. The two leading ladies, though shadowy, have well-contoured roles to perform.

Sadma

1983

Cast Kamal Haasan, Sridevi, Silk Smitha
Director Balu Mahendra
Music Ilaiyaraja
Lyrics Gulzar

Sadma tells the story of a girl who loses her memory in an accident, regresses to childhood, and is rescued and brought home by a young schoolteacher. The principal actors marvellously portray the tender, funny, sweet and bitter bond that grows between the two unlikely companions. Sridevi as the child-woman uses her squeaky voice and spectrum of expressions to full advantage. Kamal Haasan is astonishing as a man saddled with the responsibility of a child in a voluptuous woman's body. The film has stunning camerawork by director Balu Mahendra, and is rendered memorable by the two principal performances.

TIMELINE: FILMS AND LANDMARK EVENTS

1981	1981	1981	1981	1981
Khuda Kasam	Krodhi	Laawaris	Love Story	Naseeb

1961

Lata Mangeshkar's rendition of *Ae mere watan ke logon* makes an unparalleled impact as the most patriotic Indian song of all time.

Khandar

1983

Cast Naseeruddin Shah, Shabana Azmi, Anu Kapoor, Pankaj Kapur,
  Geeta Sen
Director Mrinal Sen
Music Bhaskar Chandavarkar

A National Award-winning performance by Azmi as Jamini, a bereft woman stranded in the wilderness waiting with her dying mother (the director's wife Geeta Sen) to be 'rescued.' The man who was once supposed to marry her has vanished. But when Subhash (Shah) strays into the desolation with his friends, he sparks off a ray of hope in the daughter's heart. A simple heartbreaking story of dereliction and loss written by eminent Bengali litterateur Premendra Mitra, *Khandar* was the prolific Bengali filmmaker Mrinal Sen's first feature film in Hindi. The narration moves languidly through Jamini's shattered existence creating sympathy more by implication than visual props. Though Shah is flawless in his blending into the photographer's role, *Khandar* like most Azmi starrers, is finally unforgettable for her presence. The look of forlorn grief on her face remains with us long after the film is over. This is Azmi's quietest, and according to many, most accomplished performance ever.

Both Ramesh Sippy-Amitabh Bachchan collaborations *Sholay* (1975) and *Shakti* (1982) proved to be mega hits.

1981	1981	**1981**	**1981**	1981
Professor Pyarelal	Silsila	**Subah** (See p. 148)	**Umrao Jaan** (See p. 66)	Yaarana

1962

Meena Kumari garners all the three Best Actress nominations for the Filmfare Best Actress Award: for *Aarti, Main Chup Rahoongi* and *Sahib Bibi Aur Ghulam,* for which she finally wins the award

Ghulami 1985

Cast Dharmendra, Mithun Chakraborty, Naseeruddin Shah, Reena Roy, Smita Patil, Kulbhushan Kharbanda
Director J.P. Dutta
Music Laxmikant, Pyarelal   **Lyrics** Gulzar

The epic filmmaker J.P.Dutta's romance with cinema and the Rajasthani deserts started with this forceful melodrama recreating a farmer's fight against the brutal feudal oppression in rural Rajasthan. All three protagonists played by Dharmendra, Chakraborty and Kharbanda perform within a range that goes effortlessly from subtle to dramatic. It's interesting to see how Dutta uses offbeat star Naseeruddin Shah as an antagonist, and Smita Patil as his wife who harbours an admiration for the hero's cause. Dutta's narrative was equalled by Ishwar Bidri's sweeping cinematography. The locational lyricism is matched by Laxmikant-Pyarelal's outstanding music score. In his very first film, Dutta revealed himself to be an epic visionary.

Ram Teri Ganga Maili 1985

Cast Rajeev Kapoor, Mandakini, Divya Rana, Saeed Jaffrey, Kulbhushan Kharbanda
Director Raj Kapoor
Music Ravindra Jain
Lyrics Ravindra Jain, Hasrat Jaipuri

Featuring the director's youngest son and the new discovery Mandakini, *Ram Teri Ganga Maili* chronicled the innocent and beautiful Ganga's journey from the virgin hills to the debauchery and corruption of the *kotha* (brothel) culture in Varanasi. Impregnated by a young heir (Rajiv Kapoor) who doesn't have the guts to stand up for his beloved, Ganga (Mandakini) is tossed from one place to another until the lovers are finally united. This picturesque epic was a big hit mainly for its powerful emotional story and the leading lady's generous display of her breasts. The kitschy mix of religio-political allegory and romantic melodrama took Raj Kapoor's directorial swan song to great heights of ▶ success.

TIMELINE: FILMS AND LANDMARK EVENTS

1982	1982	1982	1982	1982
Ashanti	**Bazaar** (See p. 149)	**Bemisaal** (See p. 67)	**Katha** (See p. 105)	Khuddar

1962

The Second International Film Festival is held in India.

Ijaazat

Cast Naseeruddin Shah, Rekha, Anooradha Patel
Director Gulzar
Music R.D. Burman
Lyrics Gulzar

Ijaazat is arguably the prolific and poetic filmmaker's most mature look at his favourite theme: the dynamics of the man-woman relationship. This is a triangle with a difference. There is a husband (Naseeruddin Shah), wife (Rekha) and there is the other woman. But true to her name, Maya (Anooradha Patel) is an illusory presence in the Shah-Rekha marriage. She comes and goes as she feels, creating an enchanting field of unpredictable patterns of dreams in the man's life. The film looks at the relationship between the husband and the other woman from the wife's point of view. Controlled and compelling in her dignity, Rekha is magical while Anooradha Patel (in her career's only significant role) is mystical and enigmatic. The film's highlights are R.D. Burman's songs.

Apart from Muzaffar Ali's *Umrao Jaan* (1981), *Ijaazat* (1987) is the only movie of the 1970s and '80s where Asha Bhosle did the entire music soundtrack, lending an evocative poignancy to the tale of three victims of fate trapped in a triangle where the angles are ambrosially awry.

1982	**1982**	1982	**1982**	1982
Namak Halal	**Namkeen** (See p. 68)	Prem Rog	**Saath Saath** (See p. 69)	Satte Pe Satta

(See p. 68)   (See p. 69)

1963

The Indian film industry celebrates its Golden Jubilee.

Pestonjee 1987

Cast Naseeruddin Shah, Shabana Azmi, Anupam Kher
Director Vijaya Mehta
Music Vanraj Bhatia

A very rare effort to look at the manner, speech and peculiarities of the Parsi community in Mumbai, *Pestonjee* is a love triangle about two friends and the girl whom they both love. Shah and Azmi are dead-on with their Parsi accents. The film is made memorable mainly for their performances and for the director's proclivity to prevent the Parsi people from becoming caricatural. Another standout film on the Parsi community was Pervez Mehrwanji's *Percy* released two years later. ◄

Qayamat Se Qayamat Tak 1988

Cast Aamir Khan, Juhi Chawla
Director Mansoor Khan
Music Anand, Milind
Lyrics Majrooh Sultanpuri

A fresh approach to the old theme of forbidden love and a fresh feel to the end-product. Producer Nasir Husain wrote the screenplay while son Mansoor Khan treated the familiar theme with wonder and delicacy. The director's cousin Aamir Khan was launched with great fanfare as the consummate lover-boy who falls in love with Juhi Chawla across the enemy line. The film's hot-blooded caste-ridden conflict, reminiscent of William Shakespeare's *Romeo & Juliet* gave a savage touch to the tenderness at the core. The plot built up to a shockingly tragic finale lending credence to the belief that a truly successful love story requires the lovers to come to a tragic end.

TIMELINE: FILMS AND LANDMARK EVENTS

1982	1983	**1983**	1983	1983
Shakti	Andha Kanoon	**Arth**	Avtaar	Betaab
(See p. 70)		(See p. 150)		

1964

The National Film Archives of India (NFAI) is set up in Pune.

Parinda

1989

Cast Anil Kapoor, Madhuri Dixit, Jackie Shroff, Nana Patekar
Director Vidhu Vinod Chopra
Music R.D. Burman
Lyrics Khurshid Hallauri

Chopra's unique take on Francis Ford Coppola's *The Godfather* has Shroff and Kapoor as brothers morally divided over their loyalty to the gangster Anna (Nana Patekar). Shot extensively in the film-noir style by Binod Pradhan, images from Mumbai's streets create an atmosphere of unpredictable foreboding. Gunshots mingle with the sounds of Burman's background score, as criminal elements overpower the finer aesthetics of city life. The shoot-outs, including the shocking climax where Shroff sets Patekar on fire, are staged with a keen eye for details. The violence has a choreographed edge to it.

Shroff and Kapoor played brothers or buddies in a series of films in the 1980s including *Karma* (1986) *Andar Bahar* (1989) *Ram Lakhan* (1989).

1983	1983	1983	**1983**	**1983**
Coolie	Ghungroo	Hero	**Jaane Bhi Do Yaaron** (See p. 106)	**Khandar** (See p. 71)

1964

Mehboob Khan, who directed classics such as *Andaz* (1949) and *Mother India* (1957), passes away.

Ek Doctor Ki Maut 1990

Cast Pankaj Kapur, Shabana Azmi, Irfan Khan
Director Tapan Sinha
Music Tapan Sinha

Lamhe 1991

Cast Sridevi, Anil Kapoor, Anupam Kher, Waheeda Rehman
Director Yash Chopra
Music Shiv, Hari   **Lyrics** Anand Bakshi

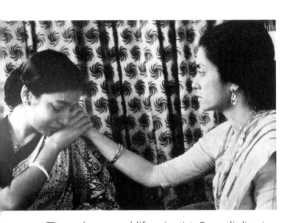

Based on a real-life scientist, Bengali director Tapan Sinha's protagonist in this small undiscovered gem of a film is a young, fiercely dedicated doctor whose passion for his profession finally destroys him. It is the story of a scientist working on a cure for leprosy who is betrayed by those close to him and finally by his own passion for the unknown. Pankaj Kapur is joined in his quest by Shabana Azmi, his supportive wife who cannot really fathom her husband's complex mind. The film is a remarkable chronicle of the mind of a genius.

Yash Chopra's personal favourite is the filmmaker's most audacious romantic outing ever. The lyrical work, hypnotically framed, packaged and filmed, tells the story of the love-smitten Anil Kapoor who loses his love (Sridevi) to another man and then to death, only to recover lost opportunity through the dead woman's daughter. The incestuous undertones in the relationship between the middle-aged man and his ex-flame's daughter severely reduced this brilliant film's viewership. But the narrative strength and the passionately packaged romance appear contemporary even today. The long medley of old evergreen songs featuring Kapoor, Sridevi and Anupam Kher culminates in the greying Waheeda Rehman dancing to her *Guide* song *Aaj phir jeene ki tamanna hai*. Fun-filled and underlined by a great intensity of vision, *Lamhe* is Yash Chopra's most lyrical and eye-catching film to date.

TIMELINE: FILMS AND LANDMARK EVENTS

1983	1983	**1983**	1983	1983
Mandi	Mangal Pandey	**Masoom**	Mazdoor	Nastik
(See p. 106)		(See p. 116)		

1964

Actor/director Guru Dutt, who directed films like *Pyaasa* (1957) *Kaagaz ke Phoo* (1959), *and Sahib Bibi aur Ghulam* (1962) , dies under tragic circumstances.

Jo Jeeta Wohi Sikandar

1992

DRAMA 77

Cast Aamir Khan, Ayesha Jhulka, Kulbhushan Kharbanda, Marmik, Deepak Tijori, Pooja Bedi
Director Mansoor Khan
Music Jatin, Lalit
Lyrics Majrooh Sultanpuri

Aamir Khan and his cousin Mansoor Khan collaborated a second time for this sporty romantic musical about a brat's coming of age. Essentially a showcase for Aamir Khan's prankish aptitudes, the film painted an idyllic landscape of the 'poor' wage-earning class (Kulbhushan Kharbanda and his two sons played by Marmik and Aamir, and the sweet little girl next door Ayesha Jhulka who is blindly devoted to Aamir) as opposed to the snooty upperclass (represented by Deepak Tijori, Pooja Bedi, and gang). Director Mansoor Khan also brought in the class act through the Aamir-Ayesha-Pooja triangle that climaxes in his realization that the rich

Pehla nasha in *Jo Jeeta Wohi Sikandar* (1992) marked Farah Khan's first path-breaking foray into choreography. More recenly, Farah has done the choreography in the hit film *Dil Chahta Hai* (2001) and even directed her own film, *Main Hoon Na* (2004).

are always self-serving. Cleverly subverting the traditional formula, the director created a work wheeling with splendid elegance to a climax where the now-sobered protagonist participates in a heart-stopping bicycle race. The sporty background accentuates the film's classy ambience.

1983	1983	1984	1984	**1984**
Sadma	Tarang	Aaj Ki Awaz	Andar Bahar	**Bhavna**
(See p. 70)				(See p. 150)

1965

Yash Chopra's *Waqt* is Bollywood's first multi-starrer.

Maya Memsaab

1992

Cast Deepa Sahi, Farooq Shaikh, Shah Rukh Khan, Raj Babbar, Paresh Rawal
Director Ketan Mehta
Music Hridayanath Mangeshkar
Lyrics Gulzar

Rudaali

1992

Cast Dimple Kapadia, Raakhee Gulzar, Raj Babbar, Raghuvir Yadav
Director Kalpana Lajmi
Music Bhupen Hazarika
Lyrics Gulzar

A fascinating adaptation of Flaubert's *Madame Bovary* created by Ketan Mehta. Playing Maya, Sahi steps into an enigmatic woman's journey into self-fulfillment. *Maya Memsaab* moves forward with a gravity- defying grace. Khan, Shaikh, Rawal and Babbar play the men in Maya's life with keen sensitivity. But it is Gulzar's poetry, the underrated Hridayanath Mangeshkar's songs and Lata Mangeshkar's singing that lift the central character to a plane of exquisite enigma. Songs like *O dil banjare, Mere sarhane jalao sapne* and *Iss dil mein bass kar dekho to* are among the most accomplished melodies of the 1990s.

An intricate study of feudalism and feminism set in the deserts of Rajasthan, *Rudaali* takes us into the life of a professional mourner, played to memorable heights of sad and dry-eyed poignancy by Dimple ► Kapadia, who is Sanicheri, the mourner who can't weep for herself. The work fuses a lyrical tone with a melodrama unique to Bengali literature (the original novel was written by eminent Bengali litterateur Maheshweta Devi) when Sanicheri runs into a feisty woman Bikhni (Raakhee). The sisterly bond between the two women gives a supple sensuous contour to the narrative.

TIMELINE: FILMS AND LANDMARK EVENTS

1984	1984	1984	**1984**	**1984**
Dharam Aur Kanoon	Ghar Ek Mandir	Karishmaa	**Paroma** (See p. 151)	**Saaransh** (See p. 152)

1965

Geeta Bali, actress from the golden age (1950s) of Bollywood passes away. Geeta became a major star after *Baazi* (1951). She went on to marry actor Shammi Kapoor.

Cast Meenakshi Sheshadri, Rishi Kapoor, Sunny Deol, Amrish Puri
Director Raj Kumar Santoshi
Music Nadeem Shravan
Lyrics Sameer

A thriller is tucked away at the epicenter of this acutely sensitive socio-drama about rape and societal responsibility. Meenakshi Sheshadri, in her career-defining role, plays a principled middle-class girl married into a capitalistic family. On a riotous day of Holi festivity *Damini* sees her brother-in-law and his friends rape the domestic help. Thus begins an epic battle between the individual and the conscience, as Damini's in-laws including her conscientious but family-obligated husband (Rishi Kapoor) try their dirtiest tricks to thwart Damini's voice of social protest. Midway into the stunning battle the fine craftsman Santoshi converts his social drama into a thriller. The arrival on the charged scene of a burnt-out alcoholic lawyer (Sunny Deol, in one of his career's better performances) signals the cinematic triumph of good over evil.

Dimple Kapadia's remarkable debut with *Bobby* (1973) established her as major teen icon. The same year, Dimple married superstar Rajesh Khanna, and did not act for twelve years. Her return, *Sagar* (1985) recast her opposite her *Bobby* co-star, Rishi Kapoor. Subsequently, Dimple went on to do more substantial roles, like in *Rudaali* (1992) which won her critical acclaim.

1984	1984	**1984**	1985	**1985**
Sautan	Sharabi	**Sparsh** (See p. 152)	Aaj Ka Daur	**Ankush** (See p. 153)

1965

Actor Motilal, famous for his role as Chunnibabu in P.C. Barua's *Devdas* (1935), passes away.

Drohkaal

1994

Cast Om Puri, Naseeruddin Shah, Amrish Puri
Director Govind Nihalani
Music Vanraj Bhatia

Roja

1994

Cast Arvind Swamy, Madhoo
Director Mani Ratnam
Music A.R. Rahman
Lyrics Mehboob

In this harsh and chilling study of the politics of terrorism Nihalani went into the bullet-ridden Kashmir valley to seek some uneasy answers to the region's militancy. The gritty plot tries to get into the head of an anti-terrorist officer (Om Puri) who takes on the might of a militant (Ashish Vidyarthi). Designed as a crackling thriller with a heart, the clenched narrative explores the psychology of terrorism to show how it affects the psyche of a battered nation.

In what turned out to be the first of his trilogy on political terrorism (followed by *Dil Se* and the Tamil *Kannathil Muttamittal*) Mani Ratnam broke into Hindi cinema with a dubbed version of this Tamil film about a wife (Madhoo) whose husband (Arvind Swamy) is kidnapped by Kashmiri militants during their honeymoon. Most of the tightly shot and edited narrative chronicles the wife's ► efforts to recover her husband. Though a success in the dubbed Hindi version much of the impact of the original Tamil is lost in translation. In the original, the wife cannot get her point across to the Hindi-speaking government officials in Tamil. That anguished collapse of communication is lost in the dubbed Hindi version. Still much of the film's patriotic zeal and political undercurrents are preserved. *Roja was* A.R. Rahman's first film assignment.

TIMELINE: FILMS AND LANDMARK EVENTS

1985	**1985**	1985	1985	**1985**
Arjun	**Ghulami** (See p. 72)	Jaan Ki Baazi	Mard	**Mirch Masala** (See p. 154)

1966

Dilip Kumar (nicknamed 'tragedy king' for his string of tragi-heroic roles) weds screen siren Saira Banu, who debuted in *Junglee* (1961).

Bombay

1995

DRAMA 81

Cast Manisha Koirala, Arvind Swamy
Director Mani Ratnam
Music A.R. Rahman
Lyrics Mehboob

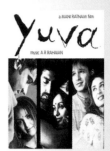

Mesmerizingly mounted, *Bombay* dared to go into a forbidden area of cinematic semantics. A Hindu-Muslim love story has always been considered taboo in our cinema. Braving the odds, Ratnam's Brahmin hero (Arvind Swamy) falls for the stunning Muslim beauty (Manisha Koirala) in the village. The couple elopes to Mumbai, only to be thrown into the simmering cauldron of communal riots that erupted in the city in 1993. There is a core of compelling conviction in the telling of the couple's journey made from innocently rebellious love to an awareness of the violence that cuts across their idyllic togetherness. Besides Mani Ratnam and Rajiv Menon's skills, the film celebrates the powerful beauty of Manisha Koirala. Looking every inch the Muslim diva, she fills the screen with an ambrosial authenticity, merging into her middle-class milieu while remaining special all the time; a quality that distinguished Madhubala many years earlier.

Following the theme of political thrillers, Ratnam made *Bombay* in 1995 and *Dil Se* in 1998. Ratnam returned to Hindi cinema six years later with *Yuva* (2004), for which a Tamil version *Ayutha Ezhuthu* (2004), has already been made with a different cast.

1985	1985	1985	1985	1986
Paar (See p. 154)	**Ram Teri Ganga Maili** (See p. 72)	Sagar	Saheb	Aakhree Raasta

(See p. 154) (See p. 72)

1966

Ritwik Ghatak becomes Director of the Film and Television Institute of India.

Rangeela

1995

Cast Aamir Khan, Urmila Matondkar, Jackie Shroff
Director Ram Gopal Varma
Music A.R. Rahman
Lyrics Mehboob

Not many films about the film industry have done well at the Indian box office. Ram Gopal Varma cast the upcoming Urmila Matondkar as the wannabe star Mili and wove a love triangle around her—a superstar (Jackie Shroff) and a street-wise petty criminal (Aamir Khan). Choreography by Saroj Khan was performed to A.R. Rahman's pulsating music. The blend brimmed over with ebullience. Varma wrote in several in-house jokes about Bollywood. The rags-to-rhythms plot was conceived and executed aesthetically. Matondkar's highly revolutionary look (designed by Manish Malhotra), body language and dance steps ushered in a new phase for Hindi cinema's leading ladies. Aamir Khan gave a gallery-pleasing performance as the Mumbai *tapori* (hoodlum).

Fire

1996

Cast Shabana Azmi, Nandita Das, Kulbhushan
　　　Kharbanda, Javed Jaffri, Ranjit Chowdhary
Director Deepa Mehta
Music A.R Rahman

Beyond the storm and fury of sensationalism caused by the lesbian theme, *Fire* is a work that dares to reach towards a higher level of expression than generally afforded to Hindi cinema. Made originally in the English language and dubbed beautifully into Hindi, *Fire* shocked the conservatives by its depiction of a physical relationship between two desperately lonely daughters-in-law, played by Shabana Azmi and Nandita Das, who belong to a business family of Delhi. Director Mehta captures household and business details in a typical Punjabi family with a captivating clutter. The dark interiors of the apartment are lit to manifest the unspoken tragedy that the house hides.

TIMELINE: FILMS AND LANDMARK EVENTS

1986	1986	1986	**1987**	**1987**
Ek Pal	Karma	Nagina	**Dacait**	**Ijaazat**
(See p. 155)			(See p. 140)	(See p. 73)

1966

Director Bimal Roy, famous for films like *Do Bigha Zameen* (1953) and *Devdas* (1956) passes away.

Cast Nana Patekar, Seema Biswas, Manisha Koirala, Salman Khan, Helen

Director Sanjay Leela Bhansali

Music Jatin, Lalit

Lyrics Majrooh Sultanpuri

This is the story of a physically challenged couple, played by Nana Patekar and Seema Biswas and their physically un-challenged daughter Manisha Koirala, whom they cling to with a desperation that almost destroys her life. Manisha, a young, emotionally frail girl is caught between the worlds of silence and music. Manisha's histrionic triumph is bolstered by an emotionally surcharged performance by Nana Patekar. As Manisha's deaf and mute father Patekar blows the screen apart with his anguish-laden performance of a kind we've never seen any male actor give in India. *Khamoshi: The Musical* holds together as an epic portrait of courage in the face of acute adversity.

Many of Patekar's raging articulations in *Khamoshi: The Musical* (1996) are expressions of director Sanjay Leela Bhansali's own angst. Bhansali used vignettes from his own memory to heighten emotional appeal—scenes between Patekar's children and their screen grandmother Helen replicate Bhansali and his sister's with their mother.

1987	1987	1987	1987	1988
Mr India	**Pestonjee**	**Pushpak**	Tezaab	Dayavan
(See p. 107)	(See p. 74)	(See p. 108)		

(See p. 107)   (See p. 74)   (See p. 108)

1966

Lyricist Shailendra who wrote the lyrics for many of Raj Kapoor's films, passes away.

Maachis

1996

Cast Tabu, Chandrachur Singh, Om Puri, Jimmy
  Shergil, Suneel Sinha, Ravi Gossain
Director Gulzar
Music Vishal Bharadwaj
Lyrics Gulzar

Gulzar's most politically vibrant film takes us straight into the rise of extremism in Punjab anti-Sikh riots after the assassination of Prime Minister Indira Gandhi in 1984. The director takes us into the life of one family ripped apart by the brutal blows of terrorism. Debutant Chandrachur Singh who plays a victim of the cruel police excesses, through the quasi-philosophical tutelage of the extremist played by Om Puri, turns to terrorism. A large part of this haunting film delineates the protagonist hiding with his fugitive friends (played by Shergil, Gossain and Sinha) in picturesque Himachal Pradesh with his devoted girlfriend (Tabu in a National Award-winning performance). The film builds up to a devastatingly tragic finale depicting the sheer futility of terrorism. One of Hindi cinema's most powerful political parables, *Maachis* saw Gulzar moving determinedly away from his characteristic lyrical style to explore a political crisis. An extraordinarily rich music score by debutant Vishal Bharadwaj (Lata Mangeshkar's *Pani pani re* shot on the outstandingly expressive Tabu remains one of the singer's most lucidly articulated songs) added to the powerful impact.

TIMELINE: FILMS AND LANDMARK EVENTS

1988	**1988**	1988	1988	1989
Khoon Bhari Maang	**Qayamat Se Qayamat Tak** (p. 74)	Raakh	Yateem	Batwara

1967

The first 70 mm wide-screen film is shown in India.

Dil Se

1998

Cast Shah Rukh Khan, Manisha Koirala, Preity Zinta
Director Mani Ratnam
Music A.R. Rahman
Lyrics Gulzar

A treatise on love during the time of terrorism, Shah Rukh and Manisha skillfully portray the desperation of a love affair conducted on borrowed time. Shah Rukh Khan as a radio journalist besotted beyond reason by an enchantingly enigmatic woman, gives one of his least stylized performances, filling those spaces in the narrative's heart with feelings that is at once rich and riveting. *Dil Se* is crowded with a compendium of thoughtful performers who support the film. Preity Zinta in her debut performance bubbles. A.R Rahman's music and Farah Khan's choreography include the celebrated *Chhaiyan chhaiyan* number on top of a moving train. Mani Ratnam's first Hindi film is a fascinating study of a sudden and

inextinguishable passion. By far the most restless Hindi film ever created, it moves from one topography and feeling to another with a desperate dexterity. In the second half of the narrative the sheer contrast between a normal bustling Delhi household during a wedding and the desolation of a female terrorist who has sacrificed all the trappings of normalcy for a cause, is brought out in passionate pastel shades.

For Preity Zinta, success came overnight. Her debut performance in *Dil Se (1998)* drew vast critical acclaim, winning her the Filmfare Award for Best Newcomer. Soon after, many films followed, including a big role in Vidhu Vinod Chopra's *Mission Kashmir* (2000).

1989	1989	1989	1989	**1989**
Chandni	Hathyar	Jaadugar	Love Love Love	**Maine Pyar Kiya**
(See p. 129)				(See p. 130)

1968

A 'Manifesto for a New Cinema' is issued by Mrinal Sen and Arun Kaul.

Kuch Kuch Hota Hai   1998

Cast Shah Rukh Khan, Kajol, Rani Mukherjee,
Sana Saeed, Farida Jalal
Director Karan Johar
Music Jatin, Lalit
Lyrics Sameer

A simple stylish, sensuous and ambrosial love story about three college friends, the film's uniquely colourful though tasteful styling by art director Sharmista Roy and costume designer Manish Malhotra furnished Johar's ultra-chic narrative with a feeling of ultimate cool with Shah Rukh Khan as the campus dude in the first half and the widower-dad in the second half. Romancing the campus siren Tina (Rani Mukherjee) or fathering the little prim-and-serious Sana Saeed, Khan's energy irrigated the roots of Johar's extremely endearing narrative. Kajol's tomboyish act took the narrative over to its second half where her character blossomed into a sari-clad seductress engaged to marry the prankish Salman Khan (in a special guest appearance) though her heart still beats for her college pal Shah Rukh Khan. Karan Johar's super-smooth treatment gives the narrative a constant flow and energy. Most of all, there's the unbeatable chemistry between Shah Rukh and Kajol. Rani Mukherjee dressed in the micro-minis sauntered her way into stardom. The packaging and projection of star charisma was unbeatable. *Kuch Kuch Hota Hai* marked the arrival of a director whose creative vision matched the size of his audience.

TIMELINE: FILMS AND LANDMARK EVENTS

1989	1989	1989	1990	1990
Parinda (See p. 75)	Pyar Ki Kahani	Ram Lakhan	Aashiqi	Agneepath

1969

Rajesh Khanna becomes India's first superstar with a string of super-hit films like *Aradhana* and *Anand*.

Satya

Cast Urmila Matondkar, Chekravarthy, Manoj Bajpai, Shefali Chhaya, Saurabh Shukla
Director Ram Gopal Varma
Music Vishal Bharadwaj
Lyrics Gulzar

One of India's most influential crime dramas, *Satya* took its astute and original director Ram Gopal Varma into the bowels of underworld crime in Mumbai. Done in a relentless documentary style, the stark visuals of violence and aggression on the swarming streets of Mumbai gave an all-new definition to the action genre in Indian cinema. All the violence was staged with the fluency and virility of real life. The characters, especially the by-now legendary Bhikhu Mhatre (played by Manoj Bajpai who catapulted to instant stardom after the rugged and raw role), project a bewildering residue of realism while remaining cinematic creatures filled with dark, uncontrollable and indefinable passions. At the centre of this lopsided crime thriller is the protagonist, Satya, played by Telugu actor Chekravarthy whose initiation and acclimatization into the world of crime takes him and the innocent middle-class girl Vidya (Matondkar, remarkably deglamourized) down.

When hotshot producer Yash Johar's son Karan Johar made his directorial debut no one expected that the film would have such a far-reaching impact. *Kuch Kuch Hota Hai* (1998) did a lot more than *kuch kuch* (something) at the box office. It was a smash hit.

1990	1990	1990	**1990**	**1990**
Anjali	Baaghi	Dil	**Ek Doctor Ki Maut**	**Ghayal**
(See p. 116)			(See p. 76)	(See p. 141)

(See p. 116)   (See p. 76)   (See p. 141)

1969

The Film Finance Corporation finances *Bhuvan Shome* (Mrinal Sen) and *Uski Roti* (Mani Kaul), both shot by K.K. Mahajan inaugurating 'New Wave Cinema.'

1947—Earth

1999

Cast Aamir Khan, Nandita Das, Rahul Khanna, Maia Seth, Kitu Gidwani, Arif Zakaria
Director Deepa Mehta
Music A.R. Rahman
Lyrics Javed Akhtar

Pakistani novelist Bapsi Sidhwa transported us to the traumatic times of India's partition in 1947 into two countries. Seen through the eyes of little Lenny (Maia Seth) *1947—Earth* spans the savage era while preserving the intimate character-study quality of Mehta's earlier work *Fire*. The love triangle among the maid Shanta (Nandita Das), her silent admirer the masseur Hassan (Rahul Khanna) and the aggressive suitor Dilnawaz (Aamir Khan) is played out at an operatic ◄ octave.

Godmother

1999

Cast Shabana Azmi, Milind Gunaji, Govind Namdeo, Sharman Joshi, Raima Sen
Director Vinay Shukla
Music Vishal Bharadwaj
Lyrics Javed Akhtar

Based on a true-life story of Ramibehn, a woman politician with more balls than her male counterparts, *Godmother* is admirably scripted by first-time director Vinay Shukla. Shabana Azmi towers over the tense plot, and the narration brings into play the politics of the Gujarati hinterland and one woman's progressive control over her political destiny. Azmi's Ramibehn falls straight into a moral cesspool to redeem herself finally by standing up against her own wayward and tyrannical son (Sharman Joshi). The taut plot builds a luminous labyrinth in Ramibehn's life. The rugged Gujarati outdoor locations and Vishal Bharadwaj's folk-tinged music score topped by Lata Mangeshkar's soul-piercing theme song *Maati re*, enchance the basic sincerity of this film about the rise and fall of a ruthlessly ambitious woman politician.

TIMELINE: FILMS AND LANDMARK EVENTS

1990	1991	1991	1991	1991
Henna (See p. 130)	Ajooba	Antarnad	Dil Hai Ki Manta Nahin	Insaaniyat

1969

The actress Madhubala, immortalized in K. Asif's *Mughal-e-Azam* (1960) dies of heart failure at the age of 36.

Fiza

Cast Jaya Bachchan, Karisma Kapoor, Hrithik Roshan, Neha, Bikram Saluja, Isha Koppiker, Asha Sachdev

Director Khalid Mohamed

Music Anu Malik, A.R. Rahman

Lyrics Gulzar, Sameer

The film's protagonists are a nuclear Muslim family. Mother Jaya Bachchan, son Hrithik Roshan and daughter Karisma Kapoor and their respective love interests (Neha and Bikram Saluja) constitute the crux of Mohamed's hardhitting film. The sister's search for her missing brother was converted into an occasion to flaunt Hrithik Roshan's brawny stardom. Karisma Kapoor pulled out all stops to deliver her career's most powerful performance. The character of the over-the-hill coquette played by Asha Sachdev, is remarkably vibrant. As the vulnerable Muslim youth whose life transforms from civil to outlaw during a communal riot, Hrithik displays a range of exquisite emotions from innocence to terror to defiance. Santosh Sivan's camerawork and the songs added considerably to the drama of dislocation.

The Kapoor family is truly the 'First Family' of Bollywood. Beginning with Prithviraj Kapoor, every generation since has produced actors and actresses—from Raj, Randhir, Shammi and Shashi Kapoor to Rishi Kapoor—and finally with the new generation, Karisma and Kareena Kapoor.

1970

Devika Rani, the 'first lady' of the Indian screen and co-owner of Bombay Talkies, is the first recipient of the Dadasaheb Phalke Award.

Kaho Na... Pyar Hai   2000

Cast Hrithik Roshan, Amisha Patel, Anupam Kher, Dalip Tahil
Director Rakesh Roshan
Music Rajesh Roshan
Lyrics Ibrahim Ashq, Sawan Kumar Tak

Filmmaker Rakesh Roshan gave his son Hrithik Roshan a double role in *Kaho Na...Pyar Hai* to showcase his acting debut. What made the two roles more interesting than usual was the fact that the characters weren't twins, long-lost (as they usually are in Hindi films) or otherwise. Hrithik played the two unrelated look-alikes with an aplomb and poise that belied his meagre experience (Hrithik had done a few films as a child). Singing, dancing, emoting and, yes, romancing debutante Amisha Patel) in the stunningly scenic locations in New Zealand and other unexplored areas, young Roshan proved himself the complete star. Would this film have worked without him? Would Paris be the same without the Eiffel Tower? Rajesh Roshan's music score, though nothing out of the ordinary on tape, came alive on screen when Hrithik emoted to *Kyun chalti hai pawan, Chand sitare* and *Ek pal ka jeena*.

TIMELINE: FILMS AND LANDMARK EVENTS

1991	1992	1992	1992	1992
Saudagar	Bekhudi	Chamatkar	Deewana	Hum

1971

The production of feature films increases to 432, making the Indian film industry the largest in the world.

Pukar

2000

Cast Anil Kapoor, Madhuri Dixit, Namrata Shirodkar
Director Raj Kumar Santoshi
Music A.R. Rahman
Lyrics Majrooh Sultanpuri, Javed Akhtar

Madhuri Dixit in a fine performance plays a girl who will go to any lengths to possess the man she loves. Set in a hill resort, *Pukar* pitched patriotism against the passions of the heart to create an arresting equipoise among the emotions of love, duty, betrayal and revenge. Santoshi's narrative style is a mixture of the traditional and the contemporary. While Dixit's powerful anti-heroine's character gives the screenplay a totally innovative dimension, Anil Kapoor's role of the dedicated soldier who, ironically, is disgraced by the woman he loves, has classic elements of drama in it. The gripping saga climaxes extraordinarily with Lata Mangeshkar appearing on screen personally to sing Rahman's composition *Ek tu hi bharosa hai* before a congregation of children amidst a terrorist attack. Though a box office failure, *Pukar* had several interesting aspects to its storytelling, most specifically Madhuri's dark-grey character that she played with ravishing relish.

Farah Khan's one dance movement where the debutant moved his hands like two fully-lit lamp shades, did the track in *Kaho Na... Pyar Hai* (2000). Hrithik Roshan's supple agility and elegance on the dance-floor made him the craze of the entire Indian populace.

1992	1992	1992	**1992**	1992
Jo Jeeta Wohi Sikandar (See p. 77)	Khuda Gawa	Mast Kalandar	**Maya Memsaab** (See p. 78)	Raju Ban Gaya Gentleman

1971

K. Asif, director of the sensational hit, *Mughal-e-Azam* (1960) passes away.

Chandni Bar

2001

Cast Tabu, Atul Kulkarni, Rajpal Yadav
Director Madhur Bhandarkar

Bhandarkar's sharply moving and extraordinarily wry film delineates the journey through life's potholes of a small-town UP girl Mumtaz who's brought to Mumbai by her uncle, and given employment as a beer-bar dancer. In one of this heart-rendingly earthy film's very real and traumatic episodes, the protagonist Mumtaz (an extraordinary brilliant Tabu) who has lost her husband and self-confidence sits with her only friend, a pimp (Rajpal Yadav) looking up and calling old clients to make some fast money for her son's release from jail. Bhandarkar's looming narrative takes his memorable protagonist from innocent abandon to unexpected hope and faith and finally plunges her into tragic and irredeemable despair.

Dil Chahta Hai

2001

Cast Aamir Khan, Akshaye Khanna, Saif Ali Khan, Preity Zinta and Dimple Kapadia
Director Farhan Akhtar
Music Shankar, Ehsan, Loy   **Lyrics** Javed Akhtar

Dil Chahta Hai is the story of three friends who grow into maturity together, losing some intrinsic values and vanity on the way. If Dil Chahta Hai can be enjoyed on one level as a perfect soufflé entertainment ▶ with outstanding performances, brilliant choreography by Farah Khan, perky songs, on another level the film's sublinear contexts regarding the choices one makes in life are weightlessly profound. Farhan Akhtar's insightfully young screenplay details the pangs in the lives of three college friends, Siddharth (Akshaye Khanna) Sameer (Saif Ali Khan) and Akash (Aamir Khan). Farhan Akhtar's film re-defines, re-aligns and re-invents several rules of popular entertainment.

TIMELINE: FILMS AND LANDMARK EVENTS

1992	1992	1993	1993	1993
Rudaali (See p. 78)	Suraj Ka Saatvan Ghoda	Baazigar	**Damini** (See p. 79)	**Darr** (See p. 124)

1971

Music composer Jaikishan of Shankar-Jaikishan fame dies.

Devdas

2002

Cast Shah Rukh Khan, Madhuri Dixit, Aishwarya Rai, Jackie Shroff, Kiron Kher
Director Sanjay Leela Bhansali
Music Ismail Durbar
Lyrics Nusrat Badr

Sanjay Leela Bhansali's adaptation of Saratchandra Chatterjee's classic romantic tragedy leaves us with a feeling of deep elation and satiation. The film requires at least two viewings to understand the visual and emotional layers that the narration secretes. Whether it is the whole elaborate ritual of bringing Devdas' two women Paro and Chandramukhi together for a mesmerizing song and dance, or the sozzled Devdas performing his own *shraddha* (last rites), Bhansali's original ideas complement and beautify the film's grand literary antecedents. The film brings a commercial grandiosity to the tale without sacrificing the original's tragic resonances. The sheer opulence of Bhansali's storytelling is unmatched by anything in any Indian film including Bhansali's own *Hum Dil De Chuke Sanam*.

The lavish Sanjay Leela Bhansali production *Devdas* (2002) is one of the most expensive films to be made in Bollywood. With a budget of close to 60 crores, everything from the opulent sets to the sumptuous costumes were made especially for the film.

1993	1993	1993	1993	1993
Hum Hai Rahi Pyar Ke	Kabhi Haan Kabhi Naa	Khalnayak	Purush	Roop Ki Rani Choron Ka Raja

1972

Chitralekha Co Op, the first co-operative started by film technicians, starts production with Adoor Gopalakrishnan's *Swayamvaram*.

Koi... Mil Gaya

2003

Cast Rekha, Hrithik Roshan, Preity Zinta
Director Rakesh Roshan
Music Rajesh Roshan
Lyrics Dev Kohli, Ibrahim Ashq,
Sayeed Naseer Faraaz

Inspired by Steven Spielberg's *ET*, *Koi...Mil Gaya* dared to demonstrate an entirely different approach of screen heroism. Playing a mentally challenged child-man who befriends an alien, Hrithik Roshan demonstrated fine control over his character's emotional landscape. Going from confused and vulnerable to a tentative strength, Roshan flaunted a strange and stirring range of expressions. The narrative was far quieter than generally seen in Rakesh Roshan's films. The mellow-drama moved in a magical mode, the leading man's interaction with his young friends, with the alien and with his romantic lead Preity Zinta (in that order) lent lustre of lyricism to the goings-on. ◄

Pinjar

2003

Cast Urmila Matondkar, Manoj Bajpai, Priyanshu
Chatterjee, Sanjay Suri, Sandali Sinha, Isha
Koppiker, Seema Biswas
Director Dr Chandraprakash Diwedi
Music Uttam Singh   **Lyrics** Gulzar

A slice of historical fiction on a par with the other great films about the Indo-Pak partition. In his maiden feature film, Diwedi has created a work timeless in its tensions and universal in appeal. From Gulzar's opening commentary to the stunning finale when the torn and traumatized protagonist Puru (Urmila Matondkar) decides to stay back with her abductor Rashid (Manoj Bajpai) in Pakistan even when offered the option of returning home to India, *Pinjar* is an enchanting tragedy that sweeps across an illimitable time and space to create a mesmeric movement of light and shade. Manoj Bajpai in the central male role of the conscience-stricken, almost penitent abductor acts without seeming to. Every actor breathes a fire of conviction into this passionately recounted tale. *Pinjar* is a film that glows with an inner conviction.

TIMELINE: FILMS AND LANDMARK EVENTS

1993	**1994**	1994	1994	1994
Sir	**1942: A Love Story** (See p. 131)	Aatish	Amanat	Andaz Apna Apna

1972

Meena Kumari passes away a few days after the release of her best-known work, *Pakeezah*.

Yuva

2004

Cast Ajay Devgan, Abhishek Bachchan, Vivek Oberoi, Esha Deol, Rani
  Mukherjee, Kareena Kapoor, Om Puri
Director Mani Ratnam
Music A.R. Rahman
Lyrics Mehboob

Yuva aspires to be a riveting blend of social message and entertainment. *Yuva* is a restless film about three young men (Devgan, Bachchan and Oberoi) who are on the look-out for a purpose in life. Among the many absorbing facets of Mani Ratnam's storytelling is the way he uses time passages in the lives of the various characters and the delightfully inventive modes of plotting whereby different perceptions are projected simultaneously into the various characters' line of vision. The 3-tiered plot creates a sense of lyricism in the plot. Every character fits in the Kolkatan milieu without stretching to cohere in the larger picture. Yet, the existence of the binding cosmic force that keeps Mani's world and the world beyond his creation looms large over the narrative. It's simply impossible to forget the three protagonists and their mesh of karmic adventures. The romantic side to the political parable about a student leader, a hit-man and a drifter is brought out so sharply in so little space, you wonder if economy of expression is Mani's mainstay as a master raconteur.

Comparisons with superstar father Amitabh Bachchan are inevitable, but Abhishek proved his mettle as a fine actor in his role as Lallan Singh in Mani Ratnam's *Yuva* (2004), for which he bagged the Filmfare Award for Best Supporting Actor.

1994	1994	**1994**	1994	1994
Anjaam	Anth	**Bandit Queen** (See p. 156)	Beta	Chand Ka Tukda

1972

More than 90% of Hindi films switch over to colour.

Black

2005

Cast Amitabh Bachchan, Rani Mukherjee, Ayesha
Kapoor, Shernaz Patel, Dhritiman Chatterjee,
Nandana Sen

Director Sanjay Leela Bhansali

Music Monty

From the extravagant grandeur and the opulent colour schemes of *Devdas,* Sanjay Leela Bhansali moved effortlessly to the minimalist shades of black and white. Veering passionately away from the norm and creating an entirely new definition of entertainment, Sanjay Leela Bhansali created a work that freezes all superlatives and permanently relocates our perceptions of high quality, intellectually and emotionally stimulating art. From the opening scene, when the blind-and-deaf Michelle (Rani Mukherjee) runs into her aged, ailing and dying teacher Debraj (Amitabh Bachchan), *Black* clamps its emotional tentacles around our hearts and refuses to release us until the end. The darkest and most inexpressible thoughts acquire shape in Bhansali's tortured and yet incredibly beautiful realm of self-expression. Credit for giving shape to his vision goes in no small measure to Bhansali's technicians who miraculously find just the right voice for the director's anguished feelings. It is impossible to imagine any other actor other than Bachchan playing Debraj, the tutor of manic proportions raging into the darkness like a Shakespearean tragic-hero. There are innumerable moments of the purest, most classical cinema in *Black*; moments such as the ones where Michelle expresses sexual yearning or when the old and dying Debraj breaks into a jig with Michelle. *Black* isn't a film that we can easily categorize. Sanjay Leela Bhansali has made history again.

TIMELINE: FILMS AND LANDMARK EVENTS

1994	**1994**	1994	**1994**	1994
Dilwale	**Drohkaal** (See p. 80)	Dulaara	**Hum Aapke Hain Koun** (See p. 117)	Hum Hai Bemisaal

1972

Prithviraj Kapoor, founder of India's first film family, the Kapoors, and actor in India's first ever talkie *Alam Ara* (1931) passes away.

एन. सी. सीप्पी कृत
हृषिकेश मुखर्जी का
चुपके
चुपके
हृषिकेश मुखर्जी · एस. डी. बर्मन
आनन्द बक्षी · गुलज़ार · जयवंत पाठारे

COMEDY

Chalti Ka Naam Gaadi 1958

Cast Ashok Kumar, Kishore Kumar, Madhubala, Anoop Kumar
Director Satyen Bose
Music S.D. Burman
Lyrics Majrooh Sultanpuri

This perennially favourite comedy is a satirical soufflé underpinned by dark, almost sinister tones of misogyny. *Chalti Ka Naam Gaadi* is zany and dangerously unpredictable in tone. While the 3 brothers indulge in a series of traffic-defying escapades on their jalopy, a rather roomy romance unfolds between the youngest sibling and a stranger who arrives on a wet and windy night to the brothers' motor garage. A lot of the romance stumbles forward in defiance of the eldest brother Ashok Kumar's strict embargo on feminine company. Apart from the quirky mixture of comedy and romance this chuckle-fest is also remarkable for a flushed and feverish soundtrack that includes several kooky Kishore Kumar canticles.

Ram Aur Shyam 1967

Cast Dilip Kumar, Waheeda Rehman, Mumtaz, Pran, Nirupa Roy
Director Tapi Chanakya
Music Naushad
Lyrics Shakeel Badayuni

One of the most emulated films of Indian cinema *Ram Aur Shyam* features the inimitable Dilip Kumar in the double role of long-lost twins. The ensuing confusions are made doubly appealing by Kumar's endearing performance. The film served as a role model for several double-role vehicles like *Seeta Aur Geeta*, *Chalbaaz* and *Kishen Kanhaiya*. This was one of Mumtaz's first big breaks as a leading lady.

TIMELINE: FILMS AND LANDMARK EVENTS

1994	1994	1994	1994	**1994**
Krantiveer	Laadla	Mammo	Milan	**Roja** (See p. 80)

1972

Playback singer Geeta Dutt, wife of actor-director Guru Dutt, dies.

Padosan

1968

Cast Sunil Dutt, Saira Banu, Mehmood, Kishore Kumar, Om Prakash
Director Jyoti Swaroop
Music R.D. Burman
Lyrics Rajinder Krishen

Considered by many connossieurs of comedy to be the funniest comic film in Hindi, *Padosan* is a courtship farce about a love-struck bumpkin's (Sunil Dutt) efforts to win the beauty next door (Saira Banu) by roping in his friend Kishore Kumar's vocal assistance. The rapidly moving plot pitches the couple's adversaries Kishore Kumar and Mehmood (playing Banu's South Indian music teacher) against each other and lets R.D. Burman's music do the rest. Songs like *Mere samne wali khidki mein*, *Kehna hai* and *Ek chatur naar* added weight to the wacky humour. Shot mostly on a set depicting two neighbouring rooms on adjacent plots the narrative's breathless humour is sustained by Kishore Kumar and Mehmod's comic timing and Burman's outstanding songs. The film's perennial popularity is undeniable.

Interestingly, the beauteous Madhubala paired romantically with both the brothers —Ashok (in Shakti Samanta's suspense thriller *Howrah Bridge,* and Kishore in *Chalti Ka Naam Gaadi,* during the same year, 1958. Her repertoire also includes *Mahal* (1949) and *Mughal-e-Azam* (1960).

1994	1995	1995	**1995**	**1995**
Saajan Ka Ghar	Akele Hum Akele Tum	Barsaat	**Bombay** (See p. 81)	**Dilwale Dulhaniya Le Jayenge** (p. 132)

1973

India's biggest star ever Amitabh Bachchan explodes on screen in *Zanjeer*.

Piya Ka Ghar

1971

Cast Jaya Bhaduri, Anil Dhawan
Director Basu Chatterjee
Music Laxmikant, Pyarelal
Lyrics Anand Bakshi

After Rajinder Singh Bedi's *Dastak* a year earlier, Basu Chatterjee's *Piya Ka Ghar* again plunged into the housing problem in Mumbai. This was the first mainstream Hindi film to be situated in a *chawl* (tenement) of Mumbai where families are packed like sardines in a tin can. Chatterjee took a quirky and quip-filled look at the marriage between a couple, Bhaduri and Dhawan, that gets seriously jeopardized because of a lack of privacy. The plot invents some seriously funny situations showing the couple's desperate attempts to be alone together. Kishore Kumar's *Yeh jeevan hai* (showing the couple's pensive mood amidst the sleeping crowds in their cramped home) and Lata Mangeshkar's *Piya ka ghar hai* (where the wife finally prepares to spend an evening alone with the husband) are remembered fondly to this day. So is Bhaduri's utterly vulnerable and endearing performance. The film came at a time when she had just begun to reign in Bollywood.

Chotisi Baat

1975

Cast Ashok Kumar, Amol Palekar, Vidya Sinha
Director Basu Chatterjee
Music Salil Chowdhury
Lyrics Yogesh

Amol Palekar, in a role that he came to specialize in, was cast as the working-class nerd who doesn't know how to approach the wholesome girl next door (Vidya Sinha). The ace up Palekar's sleeve is Ashok Kumar, the 'love tutor' who gives the nerd lessons in how to get love-savvy in a dozen easy steps. Cinematographer K.K. Mahajan shoots sequences of Palekar trailing Sinha in buses and on the roads of Mumbai with a refreshing disregard for bystanders.

TIMELINE: FILMS AND LANDMARK EVENTS

1995	1995	1995	1995	**1995**
Guddu	Karan Arjun	Oh Darling Yeh Hai India!	Ram Jaane	**Rangeela** (See p. 82)

1973

Amitabh Bachchan and Jaya Bhaduri get married.

Chupke Chupke

1975

COMEDY

101

Cast Dharmendra, Sharmila Tagore, Amitabh Bachchan, Jaya Bhaduri, Om
Prakash, Usha Kiron

Director Hrishikesh Mukherjee

Music S.D. Burman

Lyrics Anand Bakshi

One of Mukherjee's many feel-good films in the 1970s, *Chupke Chupke* is special for its impressive cast which includes the real-life pair of Bachchan and Bhaduri. The former masquerades as a botany teacher while the real botanist (Dharmendra) must masquerade as a chauffeur in his beloved's (Sharmila Tagore) home. The comedy of mistaken identity is played out with much gusto and vivacity. There are acerbic comments on the dominance of the Hindi language over all other tongues. Both Dharmendra and Bachchan, together once again after *Sholay* and *Ram Balram*, are in their comic element. Though they don't have too many scenes together their enjoyment in their Shakespearean role-exchange is evident throughout. For a Mukherjee comedy the leading ladies (both regulars in his oeuvre) have precious little to do except sing one song each about the pangs of love.

Sholay (1975) and *Chupke Chupke (1975)* revealed another facet to Dharmendra's acting—his flair for comedy! His comic timing in both films was razor sharp. He was awarded the Filmfare Lifetime Achievement Award in 1996.

1995	1995	1995	1996	1996
Trimurti	Veergati	Zamaana Deewana	Agnisakshi	Army

1973

Raj Kapoor's *Bobby* ushers in the era of the teenage love stories.

Dulhan Wohi Jo Piya Man Bhaye   1977

Cast Rameshwari, Prem Kishen, Shyamlee,
    Madan Puri, Iftekhar
Director Lekh Tandon
 Music Ravindra Jain   **Lyrics** Ravindra Jain

Known for their squeaky-clean values and wholesome family entertainers, the Rajshri banner came up with this whopper of a hit featuring newcomers. Veteran character-actor Premnath's son Prem Kishen starred as the playboy whom grandfather Madan Puri urges to marry before dying. To bring the errant grandson to heel, a masquerade of death is planned by the grandfather and his doctor-friend (Iftekhar). The plot thickens when Prem Kishen, not to be outdone by his grandfather, hires a flower seller (Rameshwari) to play his wife while he continues to romance the resident bitch (Shyamlee).

Pati Patni Aur Woh   1978

Cast Sanjeev Kumar, Vidya Sinha, Ranjeeta Kaur
Director B.R Chopra
Music Ravindra Jain
Lyrics Anand Bakshi

A comedy about a married man (Sanjeev Kumar) with roving eyes who has an affair with his secretary (Ranjeeta Kaur) and his wife's (Vidya Sinha) attempts to wean him back. The comic mood is sustained right till the end when the ostensibly errant husband flips his libido's lid again when the gorgeous Parveen Babi (making a fleeting guest appearance) walks into his office. Very few Hindi comedies before this had dared to be flippant about the sanctity of marriage and domestic values.

TIMELINE: FILMS AND LANDMARK EVENTS

1996	1996	1996	1996	**1996**
Chahat	Dastak	English Babu Desi Mem	Fareb	**Fire** (See p. 82)

1973

Heart-throb Rajesh Khanna marries teen sensation Dimple Kapadia from *Bobby* who, at 16, is 15 years younger than Khanna.

Cast Amol Palekar, Bindiya Goswami, Utpal Dutt, Dina Pathak
Director Hrishikesh Mukherjee
Music R.D. Burman
Lyrics Gulzar

A quirky and crisp comedy of errors, and a part of the amazingly prolific Mukherjee's ongoing tryst with titters in the 1970s, *Golmaal* is one of the most popular comedy films in the Hindi language. Its strength lies in the lies that the protagonist Amol Palekar tells in order to dodge his obdurate boss's (Utpal Dutt) hawk-eyed gaze. Palekar even invents his own doppelganger, thereby creating the cutest chaos seen in Hindi cinema. The pulsating performances by Palekar and Dutt hold up this ebullient comedy and give it that rush of risible rhythms that go a long way in creating situational humour. The far-reaching impact of *Golmaal* is felt in a 1990s' comedy like David Dhawan's *Coolie No.1* where the director blatantly borrowed from Mukherjee's mirth broth.

Besides its blithe, almost Shakespearean comic slant, *Dulhan Wohi Jo Piya Man Bhaye (1977)* is memorable for amiable comic performances by the two veterans Madan Puri and Iftekhar and Ravindra Jain's effervescent music score.

1996	1996	1996	1996	1996
Ghatak	Jeet	**Khamoshi: The Musical** (See p. 83)	Khiladiyon Ka Khiladi	Koyla

1973

Shyam Benegal's *Ankur* spearheads the parallel cinema movement in Bollywood.

Khubsoorat   1980

Cast Ashok Kumar, Rekha, Dina Pathak,
    Rakesh Roshan
Director Hrishikesh Mukherjee
Music R.D. Burman
Lyrics Gulzar

Among the feelgood films that the prolific Hrishikesh Mukherjee made on the theme of an outsider bringing joy into a cloistered sullen household *Khubsoorat* occupies a special place. Mukherjee cast Rekha as the 'hero' who drops into her sister's staid and repressed in-laws' residence run by the tyrannical matriarch, played by Dina Pathak. By making both the protagonist and the antagonist female figures and by making their respective male partners (Ashok Kumar and Rakesh Roshan, respectively) timid subservient creatures, this quaint comedy upholds the matriarchal order.

Chashme Buddoor   1981

Cast Farooq Shaikh, Ravi Baswani, Rakesh Bedi,
    Saeed Jaffrey
Director Sai Paranjpye
Music Raj Kamal
Lyrics Indu Jain

With this hair-down-feet-up comedy Sai Paranjpye placed herself at the centre of Bollywood's movement towards realistic comedy. Taking forward the working-class satire of Basu Chatterjee, Paranjpye here portrayed the comic camaraderie among three roommates played by Farooq Shaikh, Rakesh Bedi and Ravi Baswani. The skirt-chasing activities of the Bedi-Baswani duo occupy a major chunk of this funny and foamy film's austere footage. But it's the courtship and romance between the diffident Shaikh and the salesperson Deepti Naval (who sells detergent from door-to-door) that gives the film its delightful touch of amorous mischief. *Chashme Buddoor* worked well.

TIMELINE: FILMS AND LANDMARK EVENTS

1996	1996	1996	1996	1996
Maachis (See p. 84)	Mr Bechara	Prem Granth	Raja Hindustani	Rajkumar

1975

Ramesh Sippy's *Sholay* breaks all records at the box office and becomes the most important Hindi commercial film.

Katha

1982

Cast Naseeruddin Shah, Deepti Naval, Farooq Shaikh
Director Sai Paranjpye
Music Raj Kamal
Lyrics Indu Jain

Based on the fable of the hare and the tortoise, *Katha* gets its jumpstart quality from the exemplary trio of players playing out their titillating and tittering triangle in a chawl of Mumbai. Shah is the slow and steady suitor, while Shaikh is the roguish roving-eyed fraud. Both give performances that cover the blind spots in the narrative. Deepti Naval as the confused babe-in-the-woods is effortless. *Katha* is Paranjpye's serious attempt to study the comic nature of life in tightly cluttered tenements, earlier depicted in Basu Chatterjee's comedy *Piya Ka Ghar.*

Chashme Buddoor (1981) worked well because of the nearly untried cast. Bedi, Baswani and Saeed Jaffrey (playing a sassy paan-seller, he acquired instant acceptance in Hindi cinema) were first-rate. Shaikh and Naval formed the working-class couple in quite a few films of the 1980s including Paranjpye's *Katha* (1982).

1996	1996	1996	1996	**1997**
Saajan Chale Sasural	Salaam Bombay	Sardari Begum	Tere Mere Sapne	**Border** (See p. 112)

1975

The record-breaking mythological *Jai Santoshi Maa* is released.

Jaane Bhi Do Yaaron   1983

Cast Naseeruddin Shah, Ravi Baswani, Bhakti Barve, Om Puri, Pankaj Kapur, Satish Shah
Director Kundan Shah
Music Vanraj Bhatia

An unstoppable situational comedy with a sly touch of the slapstick. Taking into account all the mala fide forces that had gone into building that anarchic amalgamation known as Modern India, the film builds a burlesque revolving around the two protagonists' (Naseeruddin Shah and Ravi Baswani) tryst with corruption in 'high' places—the crooked builder played by Pankaj Kapur whom a scoop-hungry journalist Shobha (played by the late Barve) wants to bring to heel.

Mandi   1983

Cast Shabana Azmi, Smita Patil, Naseeruddin Shah, Om Puri, Neena Gupta, Soni Razdan, Aneeta Kanwar
Director Shyam Benegal   **Music** Vanraj Bhatia
Lyrics Bahadur Shah Zafar and Others.

Benegal added stature to his oeuvre while one of his favourite actresses added girth to her imposing personality, playing the madame of a brothel who oversees her brood of giggling, sobbing and flirtatious girls with a hawk-like ferocity. In subverting the sexual tragedy of a brothel's existence to a full-blown farce, Benegal achieved a transitional miracle within a genre that very few Hindi films have attempted. Remarkable for the gallery of women actors, the cast, particularly Naseeruddin Shah as the brothel's man Friday are deeply diverting in their drollery. The music represents the crumbling dignity of the *kotha* culture and its dominance by the more vulgar aspects of the flesh trade.

TIMELINE: FILMS AND LANDMARK EVENTS

1997	1997	1997	1997	**1997**
Chachi 420 (See p. 108)	Deewana Mastana	Dil To Pagal Hai	Gupt	**Hazaar Chaurasi Ki Maa** (See p. 156)

1975

Music composer and director S.D. Burman passes away.

Mr India
1987

Cast Sridevi, Anil Kapoor, Amrish Puri, Anu Kapoor, Satish Kaushik
Director Shekhar Kapur
Music Laxmikant, Pyarelal
Lyrics Javed Akhtar

A full-blown comic-strip on celluloid, *Mr India* and its theme of an 'invisible man' are apparently inspired by the 1964 Kishore Kumar comedy *Mr X In Bombay*. The film is produced by the leading man's brother and features him in the title role of a commoner nurturing a brood of orphans who takes on the mighty villain Mogambo (Amrish Puri). Though the caricatural conflicts between the two highlight director Shekhar Kapur's self-assured sense of the outrageous, it is Sridevi as the journalist in love with the 'invisible' hero who steals the show. Performing a parody of evergreen Laxmikant-Pyarelal songs, doing a stupendous take-off on Charlie Chaplin, dancing zanily to the comic song *Hawa Hawaii* or slithering sensuously to the orgasmic rhythms of *Kate nahin kat te* Sridevi displays a fine versatility. One of Bollywood's oldest actors Ashok Kumar made one of his final appearances as a scientist who gives the hero the potion to invisibility. Kapoor's little orphans include children who later went on to be leading man Aftab Shivdasani and choreographer Ahmed Khan.

The same team (minus director Shekhar Kapur) tried to recreate the *Mr India* (1987) magic 5 years later in the disastrous *Roop Ki Rani Choron Ka Raja* (1993) which has the dubious distinction of being the most expensive flop ever.

1997	1997	1997	1997	1997
Hero No. 1	Judwaa	Katoos	Mr and Mrs Khiladi	Mrityudand

1975

Emergency is declared by Prime Minister Indira Gandhi in June.

Pushpak

1987

Cast Kamal Haasan, Amala, Samir Kakkad,
Tinu Anand
Director Singeetham Srinivasa Rao

To this film goes the unambiguous distinction of being the only silent film in the era of talkie pictures. The ever-innovative Kamal Haasan gave one of his most striking, rich and accomplished performances as an unemployed youth who kidnaps a rich man (Kakkad). The interaction between the intended criminal and his victim involves plenty of gesticulation and miming, and absolutely no words. There's also a romance with Amala where Kamal Haasan's ability to articulate thoughts without words are most at work.

Chachi 420

1997

Cast Kamal Haasan, Tabu, Amrish Puri, Om Puri,
Paresh Rawal, Ayesha Jhulka
Director Kamal Haasan
Music Vishal Bharadwaj   **Lyrics** Gulzar

In *Chachi 420*, Tamil Nadu's resident maverick Kamal Haasan gets into a buxom Maharashtrian's garb to play nanny to his two kids after separating with his wife. *Chachi 420* is a wittily written piece of comedy with humour that braces even as the narrative races towards a wackily worked-out finale. The film has a large supporting cast including Om Puri, Amrish Puri and Paresh Rawal who are completely convincing in their comic comportment. Veteran comedian Johnny Walker made his last screen appearance as an inebriated make-up person who facilitates the protagonist's transition into femininity. Finally, the film is a made-to-order vehicle for the amazing Kamal Haasan. Playing a warm matronly woman the actor gets into the skin of the character for the most convincing drag act since Dustin Hoffman in *Tootsie*. The film was initially directed by admaker Shantanu Sheorey before Kamal Haasan took over the job.

TIMELINE: FILMS AND LANDMARK EVENTS

1997	1997	1997	1997	1998
Mrityudaata	Pardes	Viraasat	Yes Boss	Achanak

1976

Emergency results in strict censorship of films—*Kissa Kursi Ka*, a political satire directed by Amrit Nahata, is destroyed.

WAR DRAMA

Dr Kotnis Ki Amar Kahani

1946

Cast V. Shantaram, Jayshree **Director** V. Shantaram
Music Vasant Desai **Lyrics** Dewan Sharar

The film opens with Dr Kotnis (director Shantaram) returning to his native village to convince his parents that he is needed in China, where Japan's aggression has left many wounded. Once in China, the narrative wastes no time in turning into an Indo-China romance with Dr Kotnis spending more time courting and flirting with a Chinese girl (played by the director's wife Jayashree) than curing the locals in China who speak Hindi, albeit with a Chinese accent! *Dr Kotnis…* rises above the quirky crassness of the kitschy content on the strength of its noble theme and intention and Shantaram's remarkably textured and emotionally rich performance.

Hum Dono

1961

Cast Dev Anand, Sadhana, Nanda
Director Amarjeet
Music Jaidev
Lyrics Sahir Ludhianvi

Produced by Dev Anand's illustrious Navketan banner, this film about mistaken identity created a box office stir of sorts. Improbable, yet engrossing, *Hum Dono* tells the story of two 'identical non-twins,' both in the army and battling a common enemy. When one of them is presumed dead at war the other one must return home to pose as the widow's (Nanda) husband. The 'missing-in-action' formula created a heady drama. The film was supported by a superlative music score by Jaidev. Dev Anand in the two roles, with and without a moustache, is the consummate romantic wishing away all his worries in a haze of smoke.

TIMELINE: FILMS AND LANDMARK EVENTS

1998	1998	1998	1998	1998
Angaarey	Aunty No. 1	Bade Miyan Chote Miyan	Baadshah	Bandhan

1976

Legendary playback singer Mukesh dies.

Haqeeqat

1964

Cast Dharmendra, Balraj Sahni, Priya Rajvansh, Vijay Anand, Jayant
Director Chetan Anand
Music Madan Mohan
Lyrics Kaifi Azmi

Haqeeqat, recreating the torment of the Indo-China war in 1962, is to this date one of Bollywood's most authentic depictions of battle fatigue. Shot on location in Ladakh, the bleak non-judgmental landscape is shot in exquisite black and white. The soldiers, played with understated machismo added lustre of credibility to an already-authentic narrative. Chetan Anand wove a touching romance into the wartime exigencies with debutant Priya Rajvansh as a rural belle who helps the Indian soldiers fight off the Chinese menace. The film is suffused in patriotism and nostalgia, qualities that are accentuated by Kaifi Azmi's lyrics and Madan Mohan's compositions.

Guru Dutt's directorial debut, *Baazi* (1951) starred his good friend Dev Anand. When they first met at Prabat Studios in 1945, they promised to work together if Dev was to turn producer and Guru Dutt was to turn director. However, it was films like *Hum Dono* (1961) and *Guide* (1965) which shot Dev Anand to fame.

1998	1998	1998	1998	**1998**
Barood	China Gate	Devta	Dhoondte Reh Jaaoge	**Dil Se** (See p. 85)

1980

Playback singer Mohammad Rafi, whose golden voice graced scores of Bollywood films, passes away.

Border

1997

Cast Sunny Deol, Jackie Shroff, Suniel Shetty, Akshaye Khanna, Tabu, Pooja Bhatt, Raakhee Gulzar
Director J.P. Dutta
Music Anu Malik
Lyrics Javed Akhtar

J.P. Dutta, whose brilliant craftsmanship was on display in his earlier works (*Ghulami, Batwara, Hathyar*), pulled out all stops to make *Border* a brilliant war epic. Set during the 1971 Indo-Pak war, *Border* unfolds in episodic bouts of battle-front flare-ups pitched at a level of technical finesse that made these the most authentic war sequences ever filmed in Indian cinema. But it is the characters that grip you. Each soldier, from the turbaned Sunny Deol to the callow Akshaye Khanna recalls more peaceful and romantic times away from the boom of the canons. The soundtrack, a sturdy mix of war sounds and Anu Malik's tonic music is a prescription for introspection. The brilliantly devised film interweaves war and romance into a passionate pastiche. The performances are all uniformly even-toned. Dutta's inner convictions manifest in rugged sharp-toned images and dialogues that take the war genre in cinema where it had never gone before.

1980

Sahir Ludhianvi, lyricist for films like *Pyaasa* (1957) and *Hum Dono* (1961), passes away.

Hum Aapke Hain Koun..!

Gumrah

1963

Cast Ashok Kumar, Mala Sinha, Sunil Dutt, Shashikala
Director B.R. Chopra
Music Ravi
Lyrics Sahir Ludhianvi

When Sunil Dutt sang Sahir's sublime words to Mala Sinha, time—and love—stood still. In this provocative drama the socially conscientious filmmaker B.R. Chopra continued his exploration of social issues. *Gumrah* was about marriage, fidelity and the sanctity of domesticity. Chopra's leading lady Mala Sinha was compelled to marry her dead sister's husband Ashok Kumar. Shockingly, she continued to meet her lover Sunil Dutt. Undercurrents of defiant direction drive the high-voltage drama. Shashikala who plays the blackmailer walked away with the Filmfare Award for her shrewish performance.

Avishkar

1973

Cast Rajesh Khanna, Sharmila Tagore
Director Basu Bhattacharya
Music Kanu Roy
Lyrics Kapil Kumar

In his marital trilogy—*Anubhav, Avishkar and Grihapravesh*—the filmmaker explored the anatomy, psychology and politics of marriage with a splendid eye for physical and emotional details. In *Avishkar* he got the two glamorous stars, Rajesh Khanna and Sharmila Tagore to play the archetypal couple Amar and Mansi, squabbling bitterly after some years of marriage, as disillusioned with marriage as they are with the rites of remaining silent in an alliance that has gradually been stripped of all appeal and meaning.

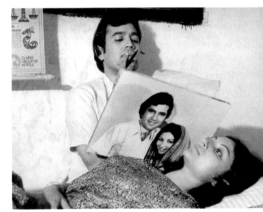

TIMELINE: FILMS AND LANDMARK EVENTS

1998	1998	1998	1998	1998
Ghulam	Gunda	Hero Hindustani	Hyderabad Blues	Jab Pyar Kisise Hota Hai

1980

Actress Hema Malini becomes Dharmendra's second wife. Hema Malini and Dharmendra are remembered for their fabulous chemistry in Ramesh Sippy's hit film *Sholay*.

Bidaai

Cast Jeetendra, Leena Chandavarkar, Durga Khote
Director L.V. Prasad
Music Laxmikant, Pyarelal
Lyrics Anand Bakshi

Remarkable for his prolific output the Tamil-Telugu-Hindi movie moghul L.V. Prasad made this melodrama as a tribute to the joint family. Fragmentation due to the migration that results from the post-Independence generation's craving for a better life forms the core of the drama. One by one, village matriarch Durga Khote loses her entire family to the city until she's left in the ancestral home to die alone. In a providential twist of fate, her grandson finds his way back to the village to redeem the grandmother's dying days. Hallucinating at death's door the old lady sees the grandson as Lord Krishna who has come to salvage her soul. The blend of mythology and cultural exposition underlined the film's main theme. The film is also remarkable for casting the screen matriarch Durga Khote in the pivotal role, and Leena Chandavarkar as her shrewish daughter-in-law who entices the old lady's favourite son (Jeetendra) away from his mother.

In the late 1960s and early '70s, Sharmila Tagore and Rajesh Khanna sizzled on screen with a string of hits. The films served to propel Rajesh Khanna into superstardom.

1998	1998	1998	**1998**	1998
Jhoot Bole Kauwa Kaate	Kaalicharan	Kareeb	**Kuch Kuch Hota Hai** (See p. 86)	Kudrat

1981

Legendary actress Nargis who acted in films like *Andaz* (1949) and *Mother India* (1957) dies five days before the premiere of her son Sanjay Dutt's debut film, *Rocky*.

Masoom

1983

Cast Naseeruddin Shah, Shabana Azmi, Jugal Hansraj,
Urmila, Aradhana, Saeed Jaffrey, Tanuja
Director Shekhar Kapur
Music R.D. Burman   **Lyrics** Gulzar

Shekhar Kapur's directorial debut was a sensitive story about the troubles a happily married couple face after the arrival of the husband's illegitimate son from a past affair. Kapur converted the inherently sentimental tale into a gripping and gentle urban fable. Shabana plays the wife who gradually comes to terms with her husband's slip-up.

Anjali

1990

Cast Raghuvaran, Revathi, Baby Shyamali
Director Mani Ratnam
Music Ilaiyaraja

Tamil maverick Mani Ratnam's breakthrough in the Hindi cinema was a dubbed version of his lyrical and moving fable about a young mentally challenged girl (Baby Shyamali) who is brought home to her family for a normal life. The ebullient girl's initiation into the family includes a large number of smartly executed dance numbers replicating the in-your-face grace and frenzied pace of the music videos from the West. This was the first Indian film to actually go into Westernized choreography. It did so without losing focus on the Indianness in the texture of the emotions depicted. The cast of youngsters led by Baby Shyamali were delightfully natural. In its vitality of emotions *Anjali* was a complete path-breaker. A heart-wrenching portrayal of strength within fragility *Anjali* was made into Tamil and dubbed into Hindi. The quality and tone of the emotions, the artless wonderment of discovering life in all its glory, gave a universal resonance to the narration.

TIMELINE: FILMS AND LANDMARK EVENTS

1998	1998	1998	1998	1998
Maharaja	Main Solah Baras Ki	Major Saab	Mehendi	Mere Do Anmol Ratan

1981

Sanjay Dutt, son of actress Nargis and actor Sunil Dutt, debuts in the highly anticipated *Rocky*. It is a great commercial success.

Hum Aapke Hain Koun

Cast Salman Khan, Madhuri Dixit, Anupam Kher, Renuka Shahane,
Mohnish Behl, Reema Lagoo
Director Sooraj Barjatya
Music Ram Laxman
Lyrics Dev Kohli, Ravinder Rawal

Rajshri Production house styled what is undoubtedly one of the 3 most successful Hindi films of all times. *Hum Aapke...* is a film about 'family values' with nearly 3.5 hours of elaborate song and dance sequences and the situations that require them! These include a long wedding ceremony where the rituals spread themselves out over two songs until the bride (Renuka Shahane) leaves for her husband's (Mohnish Behl) home. The main event in the commodious plot concerns the romance that blossoms between Shahane's sprightly younger sister Madhuri Dixit and the groom's obedient but bratty brother Salman Khan. While the two frolic with arcadian innocence, various festive celebrations supported by Ramlaxman's kitschy songs and Jay Borade's ornate choreography come and go in swaying cyclic motions of joint-family routine. Tragedy strikes, albeit briefly, creating a dramatic pause in the film. What sees the film through is its amazing lack of guile. The 'Indian' values are placed within a modern context.

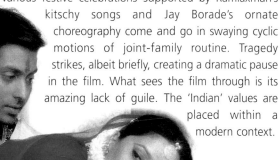

Urmila Matondkar and Aradhana as Shabana and Shah's daughters in *Masoom* (1983) gave the most natural performances seen by children in mainstream Hindi cinema. Jugal Hansraj as the little heartbreaker who unknowingly disrupts a home and marriage was especially endearing.

1998	1998	1998	1998	1998
Naseeb	Pardesi Babu	Prem Agan	Pyar Kiya To Darna Kya	Pyar To Hona Hi Tha

1982

India's greatest screen icon Amitabh Bachchan has a near-fatal accident on the sets of Manmohan Desai's *Coolie*.

Kabhi Khushi Kabhie Gham

2000

Cast Amitabh Bachchan, Jaya Bachchan, Shah Rukh Khan, Kajol, Hrithik Roshan, Kareena Kapoor, Rani Mukherjee, Farida Jalal, Alok Nath, Johnny Lever
Director Karan Johar
Music Jatin, Lalit, Sandesh Shandilya
Lyrics Sameer, Anil Pandey

Karan Johar scaled the pinnacle of pop-entertainment in his debut film *Kuch Kuch Hota Hai*. In *Kabhi Khushi Kabhie Gham* (*K3G*) he goes even further to extend the parameters of his creative vision while stretching the frontiers of feel-good mass-oriented entertainment in Hindi cinema. *K3G* is about Hrithik's search for his brother (Shah Rukh Khan) who was disowned by their father. The conventional plot replete with every conceivable formulaic bait from slick comedy in Delhi's Chandni Chowk area (courtesy Kajol) to chic sensuality in London (courtesy Kareena Kapoor), is given an incredibly sumptuous eye-catching spin by the second-time director. Johar leaves no stone unturned to ensure a smooth sailing triumphant journey for *K3G* across the global box office. Kajol and Shah Rukh Khan, specially the former, have the author-backed roles. They make the best of the plot's dramatic convergence on their characters. Johar invests every scene with a certain emotional high so that the film is actually an amalgamation of a series of implosive climaxes.

TIMELINE: FILMS AND LANDMARK EVENTS

1998	**1998**	1998	1998	1998
Samar	**Satya** (See p. 87)	Sher Khan	Soldier	Terrorist

(See p. 87)

1982

Bhanu Athaiya is the first Indian to win an Oscar for her costumes in Richard Attenborough's *Gandhi,* in which Ben Kingsley immortalized the role of M.K. Gandhi.

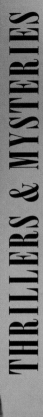

Mahal 1949

Cast Ashok Kumar, Madhubala
Director Kamal Amrohi
Music Khemchand Prakash
Lyrics Nakshab

A turning point in the career of both the 'ghost' Madhubala and her ghost-voice Lata Mangeshkar, *Mahal* has become synonymous with the supremely sonorous *Aayega aanewala* song that gave birth to the cult of ethereal and melodious spirits haunting heroes of our films. *Mahal* is a hugely tangled supernatural thriller about a man, played by Ashok Kumar and his obsession with an apparition that drives his wife to suicide and him to the brink of insanity.

Kohraa 1964

Cast Biswajeet, Waheeda Rehman, Lalita Pawar
Director Hiren Nag
Music Hemant Mukherjee
Lyrics Kaifi Azmi

*K*ohraa featured the ethereal Waheeda Rehman as the mysterious rake Biswajeet's second wife who's haunted by his dead wife. The chilling ambience was sublimated by the producer Hemant Mukherjee's vintage music. Songs like Lata Mangeshkar's *Jhoom jhoom dhalti raat* and *O beqaraar dil* heightened the feeling of ominous dread in the plot. Montages of the dead woman's spirit wandering the night were exquisitely expressive. Waheeda Rehman as the Indian version of Rebecca was vulnerable, adamant and very beautiful. This is one of the superior supernatural thrillers of the 1960s where the actors respond to a particular plot rather than peripheral attractions such as songs and romance.

TIMELINE: FILMS AND LANDMARK EVENTS				
1998	1998	1998	1998	1998
Wajood	Yamraj	Zakhm	Zakhmee Aurat	Zanjeer

1982

The Asian Games held in New Delhi provide the occasion to start telecasting TV programmes in colour.

Cast Ashok Kumar, Dev Anand, Vyjanthimala, Tanuja
Director Vijay Anand
Music S.D. Burman
Lyrics Majrooh Sultanpuri, Shailendra

A film about mistaken identity starring the debonair Dev Anand cast as look-alikes. This clever suspense film with a surfeit of skilful narrative devices all climaxing in one of the most heart-stopping song-and-dance sequences ever filmed (*Hothon pe aisi baat*) is still a whopper of an entertainer. A masala mix, well-oiled though not over-spiced, pickled with the pride of the formulaic menu. S.D. Burman's music goes a long way in embellishing and heightening the theme and mood. Interestingly, the second lead Tanuja (seducing her man with Asha Bhosle's seductive *Raat akeli hai*) looks far more comfortable with the hero than the heroine Vyjanthimala. The stiff mood between the lead pair goes well with the plot. *Jewel Thief* is the kind of film where everything including the suspense, just falls into place with a rustling grace.

Although Madhubala had been a heroine for a couple of years, *Mahal* (1949) finally made her a star. Madhubala had been a child star in one of Bombay Talkies' biggest hits, *Basant (1937)*. Five years later, she was playing the exquisitely beautiful heroine opposite the studio's top actor, Ashok Kumar.

1998	**1999**	1999	1999	1999
Zulmositam	**1947—Earth** (See p. 88)	Arjun Pandit	Biwi No. 1	Chehera

1984

Sohrab Modi, director of films like *Pukar* (1931), *Sikander* (1941) and *Sheesh Mahal* (1950), passes away.

Ittefaq
1969

Cast Nanda, Rajesh Khanna
Director Yash Chopra
Lusic (background score) Salil Chowdhury

The ever-experimental B.R.Chopra produced this songless thriller, his second film after the courtroom drama *Kanoon*. The raw and riveting Rajesh Khanna played a man accused of murdering his wife who takes asylum in a single woman's (Nanda) home and finds himself a part of a much bigger more damning conspiracy than he could have ever imagined. The taut whodunit moves at a frenetic speed. Director Yash Chopra never allows the narrative to stray. Most of the stagey film is shot on one set depicting Nanda's home. The dramatic tension is created mainly through the editing pattern and the principal performances. Rajesh Khanna is outstanding in his outbursts of defensive anger and uncontrollable rage. But the real shocker is Nanda. Turning away from her goody-goody image she delivers a sledgehammer performance as a scheming, screaming evil woman of devious devices. There is not a hint of romance in the plot. *Ittefaq* is a genre-defining work.

TIMELINE: FILMS AND LANDMARK EVENTS

1999	1999	**1999**	1999	1999
Dil Kya Kare	Dillagi	**Godmother** (See p. 88)	Hasina Maan Jayegi	Hello Brother

1985

Shiva Ka Insaf, the first 3-D feature film in Hindi is released.

Lekin

1991

Cast Vinod Khanna, Dimple Kapadia, Amjad Khan
Director Gulzar
Music Hridayanath Mangeshkar
Lyrics Gulzar

Produced by 'Asia's Nightingale' Lata Mangeshkar, *Lekin* is a ghost story with a difference. *Lekin* transports us into the twilight 'now-you-see-her-now-you-don't' zone. Frozen between two lives the female protagonist's character is guided by the hero Vinod Khanna from one world to another—a symbolic journey represented by a splendid stretch of sand which cinematographer Manmohan Singh captures with undulating elasticity. Gulzar's vision lends a lyrical

In the 1960s, B.R. Chopra made two successful songless films: *Kanoon* (1960), starring Mehmood and *Ittefaq* (1969) starring Rajesh Khanna and Nanda.

luminosity to the epic tale. The film is made memorable by Dimple Kapadia's unblinking portrayal of the ghost, rendered immeasurably ethereal by the underrated composer Hridayanath Mangeshkar's haunting melodies sung with ravishing resonance by the composer's sister Lata Mangeshkar.

1999	1999	1999	**1999**	1999
Hindustan Ki Kasam	Hote Hote Pyar Ho Gaya	Hu Tu Tu	**Hum Dil De Chuke Sanam** (See p. 133)	Hum Saath Saath Hain

1985

Actor Sanjeev Kumar, who acted in films like *Sangharsh* (1968), *Khilona* (1970) and *Koshish* (1972), passes away.

Darr

Cast Sunny Deol, Juhi Chawla, Shah Rukh Khan
Director Yash Chopra
Music Shiv, Hari
Lyrics Anand Bakshi

Making a departure from the ultra-romanticism of *Daag, Kabhi Kabhie* and *Chandni,* Yash Chopra swerved fluently into the sinister with this film. As the psychologically disturbed lover-boy who can't take no for an answer from Juhi Chawla, Shah Rukh Khan made a fashion statement out of stammering manic love-confessions. Though the film was packaged as a typical Yash Chopra romance

(with dulcet melodies composed by the classical musicians Shiv Kumar Sharma and Hari Prasad Chaurasia and sung by Lata Mangeshkar projected into an alfresco Alpine environment) *Darr* was also a scare-fest, with Shah Rukh jumping at Juhi from the most unlikely places. While the hero, Deol was impressive enough in his macho manoeuvres, his adversary who would be traditionally termed the villain, was turned into an attractive figure. Evil became attractive and danger was fun. Especially remarkable are the film's editing patterns, which create suspense in unexpected sequences. The long Holi sequence where Shah Rukh infiltrates the festivities at Deol-Chawla's home and the chase on the crowded roads thereafter, are deviously executed.

TIMELINE: FILMS AND LANDMARK EVENTS

1999	1999	1999	1999	1999
Hum Tum Pe Marte Hain	Jaanam Samjha Karo	Janwar	Kartoos	Kaun

1986

Actress Smita Patil, known for her contribution to parallel cinema and films such as *Bhumika* (1977), *Bazaar* (1982) and *Mandi* (1983), dies at age 31.

ROMANCE

yashchopra's
Kabhi
Kabhie
Love is Life
eastmancolor
SAGAR SARHADI
LYRICS SAHIR

Bobby   1973

Cast Rishi Kapoor, Dimple Kapadia, Premnath, Pran,
    Sonia Sahni, Durga Khote, Aruna Irani, Prem
    Chopra, Farida Jalal
Director Raj Kapoor
Music Laxmikant, Pyarelal   **Lyrics** Anand Bakshi

With his second son Rishi and the 15-year
-old sensation Dimple in the lead, Raj
Kapoor made a romantic saga based on
Shakespeare's *Romeo & Juliet*. Pran and Sonia
Sahni neglect their only son Raja (Rishi Kapoor).
Deeply attached to his nanny (Durga Khote)
Raja grows into his teens to promptly fall in
love with the nanny's granddaughter Bobby
(Dimple Kapadia). While her boorish dad
(Premnath) and Raja's upper-class father fight a
pitched class battle, Raja romances Bobby.

Julie   1975

Cast Laxmi, Vikram, Om Prakash, Nadira,
    Jalal Agha
Director K.S. Sethumadhavan
Music Anand Bakshi, Harindranath Chattopadhyay
Lyrics Rajesh Roshan

Julie was a trend-setting romance depicting a
'forbidden' and largely doomed relationship
between an Anglo-Indian girl (Laxmi) and a
Hindu boy (Vikram). Done with a daredevil
sensuality, then unknown to mainstream Hindi
cinema, the romance was further garnished
with Rajesh Roshan's path-breaking ballads like
Julie I love you and *Dil kya kare*. The film was
shot close to the railway
tracks giving the film a
texture of authenticity
lacking in the main
romance, with its
over-blown
emotions. What
gave the female
protagonist's
routine romance
an extra edge was
the daring pre-
marital pregnancy.

TIMELINE: FILMS AND LANDMARK EVENTS

1999	1999	1999	1999	1999
Kohram	Kya Kehna	Mann	Mast	Rockford

1987

Actor and playback singer, Kishore Kumar, passes away.

Cast Amitabh Bachchan, Raakhee, Shashi Kapoor, Waheeda Rehman, Rishi Kapoor, Neetu Singh, Simi Garewal, Pariskhat Sahni, Naseem
Director Yash Chopra
Music Khayyam
Lyrics Sahir Ludhianvi

Arguably the most intensely romantic film by Yash Chopra, *Kabhi Kabhie* was the inspiration for Karan Johar's *Kabhi Khushi Kabhie Gham*. Its elaborate plot serves as a subtle game of musical chairs for two ill-matched couples, the poet Amit (Bachchan) who loves Pooja

(Raakhee) actually marries another woman (Waheeda Rehman) while Pooja is married to a well-meaning though prosaic man (Shashi Kapoor) who can make her happy but cannot make his wife forget her first love. The overlapping relationships were played out against a stunningly scenic backdrop. The title song by Lata Mangeshkar is timeless in its lyrical luminosity.

The mother of all the teen-romances that thereafter flooded filmdom, *Bobby (1973)* marked the return of the showman par excellence, Raj Kapoor, to voluptuous form after the failure of *Mera Naam Joker (1971)*. Dimple Kapadia activated a *Bobby* blizzard in India—her uninhibited display of teen spirit and her no-holds-barred dancing made her the first teen icon of Bollywood.

1999	1999	1999	1999	1999
Sarfarosh	Shiva	Shool	Sooryavansham	Taal

1987
Music composer Shankar of Shankar-Jaikishan fame, passes away.

Laila Majnu

1977

Cast Rishi Kapoor, Ranjeeta Kaur, Danny Denzongpa
Director H.S. Rawail
Music Madan Mohan, Jaidev
Lyrics Sahir Ludhianvi

A love legend with a lyrical underbelly. At least 12-13 film versions chronicling the legendary romance between Qais and Laila have been attempted in Indian cinema. H.S. Rawail whose earlier success with love stories within the costume-drama genre (*Mere Mehboob, Sangharsh*) created a gripping case for Qais and Laila's forbidden love. Rishi Kapoor re-living the life of the demented lovelorn character implanted an epic chip on this film's broad shoulders. With the deep-throated Mohammad Rafi singing soul-piercing love ballads, Kapoor made the ideal legendary lover.

Ek Duuje Ke Liye

1981

Cast Kamal Haasan, Rati Agnihotri, Swapna
Director K. Balachander
Music Laxmikant, Pyarelal
Lyrics Anand Bakshi

Tamil maverick Kamal Haasan's outstanding Hindi debut starred him as a Tamilian who falls in love with his Punjabi neighbour, played with spirited passion by debutante Rati Agnihotri. The romantic liaison was strewn with some splendid linguistic confusions and, of course, parental opposition, including Shobha Khote as the girl's draconian mother bullying the young couple into a one-year separation that ends in tragedy. Balchander's Hindi debut was a hands-on full-blast melodrama replete with one of the best music scores ever composed for a Hindi film.

TIMELINE: FILMS AND LANDMARK EVENTS

1999	1999	**2000**	2000	2000
Thakshak	Vaastav	**Astitwa** (See p. 157)	Baaghi	Badal

1988

India's greatest showman Raj Kapoor passes away one month after receiving the prestigious Dadasaheb Phalke award.

Chandni

Cast Sridevi, Rishi Kapoor, Vinod Khanna, Waheeda Rehman
Director Yash Chopra
Music Shiv, Hari
Lyrics Anand Bakshi

Tailored to accommodate the considerable charisma and star power of Sridevi, *Chandni* marked the return of Yash Chopra. In *Chandni* he worked a mellifluent magic with Sridevi, presenting her as the ultimate dream-woman whom men fantasize about while their mothers see the ideal daughter-in-law in her. The mixture of voluptuary and vulnerability was potent. *Chandni* is the story of a romance gone wrong and redeemed in the nick of time by a quirky twist of fate. The two men in Chandni's life (played by Rishi Kapoor and Vinod Khanna) are brilliantly shadowy, complementing the heroine's awesome screen presence. The film is timeless not so much for its story content or treatment, but the director's exemplary aesthetic sense matched by his leading lady's breathtaking screen presence.

Laila Majnu (1977) was one of the many films Rishi Kapoor did. Dimple Kapadia in *Bobby* (1973) Kajal Kiran in *Hum Kissi se Kum Nahin* (1977) and Jaya Prada in *Sargam* (1979) and Shoma Anand in *Barood* (1998) were some others who made their debut with this versatile actor.

2000	2000	2000	2000	2000
Bulundi	Beti No. 1	Bichhoo	Chal Mere Bhai	Champion

1989

Ashok Kumar receives the Dadasaheb Phalke Award.

Maine Pyar Kiya   1989

Cast Salman Khan, Bhagyashree, Mohnish Behl, Alok Nath, Reema Lagoo, Ajit Vachchani
Director Sooraj Barjatya
Music Ram Laxman
Lyrics Asad Bhopali, Dev Kohli

Launching the super-successful career of director Sooraj Barjatya and his leading man Salman Khan, *Maine Pyar Kiya* spawned a whole ethos of teenybopper romantic musicals in the 1990s. The rich Prem (Khan) wooed, won, almost lost and won back the young, working-class girl Suman (Bhagyashree). Unconventionally, the courtship takes place with bumper-sticker poetry and dime-store jingle songs within the boy's home where the girl is a ◀ house guest. Barjatya's joint-family romance broke innumerable records.

Henna   1990

Cast Rishi Kapoor, Zeba Bakhtiar, Ashwini Bhave, Saeed Jaffrey, Farida Jalal
Director Raj Kapoor
Music Ravindra Jain
Lyrics Ravindra Jain

Movie moghul Raj Kapoor had a dream. He wanted to make a symbolic love story where the two traditional enemies India and Pakistan came together in a romantic clasp. He died before his dream could be fulfilled. But his son Randhir Kapoor took over the dream, and did a rather fine job of weaving a gossamer romance between an Indian boy (Rishi Kapoor) who strays into Pakistan after losing his memory and falls in love with a tribal Pakistani girl, played by debutante Zeba Bakhtiar. *Henna* worked as a comment on Indo-Pak amity long before it became a fashionable political statement. Randhir Kapoor shot the film in verdant stretches of unspoilt landscapes.

TIMELINE: FILMS AND LANDMARK EVENTS

2000	2000	2000	**2000**	2000
Deewane	Dhadkan	Dulhan Hum Le Jayenge	**Fiza** (See p. 89)	Gaja Gamini

1989

The first Bombay International Festival of Short Films and Documentaries is held.

1942: A Love Story 1994

Cast Anil Kapoor, Manisha Koirala, Jackie Shroff, Chandni, Anupam Kher,
Manohar Singh, Sushma Seth
Director Vidhu Vinod Chopra
Music R.D. Burman
Lyrics Javed Akhtar

An idyllic satiny love story set amidst the tumult of the Quit India movement before India's Partition, *1942...*is a mellow melodious picnic into an era of panic. Chopra synthesizes historical facts with his romantic vision without compromising on the quality of credibility. From the time the apolitical Anil Kapoor sets his eyes on the beauteous Manisha Koirala the narrative chalks out a charming path for a liaison that's qualified by the politics of the times. The songs and their filming are very special. In R.D. Burman's last remarkable score (for which director Chopra coaxed him out of a black unsuccessful period of semi-exile) Burman came up with a score with scintillating contours. Songs like *Kuch na kaho, Ek ladki ko dekha* and *Pyar hua chupke se* enhanced the innate romanticism of the tale. Some song situations were conceived and filmed by one of today's foremost filmmakers Sanjay Leela Bhansali.

Bhagyashree, the leading lady of *Maine Pyar Kiya* (1989) was an overnight sensation but faded away soon after, lending credence to the belief that only one of two debutantes in a romantic film is successful— Karisma Kapoor and Hareesh in *Prem Qaidi* (1991); Manisha Koirala and Vivek Mushran in *Saudagar* (1991); Madhoo and Ajay Devgan in *Phool Aur Kante* (1992) and Kajol and Kamal Sadanah in *Bekhudi* (1992).

2000	2000	2000	**2000**	2000
Hamara Dil Aapke Paas Hai	Har Dil Jo Pyar Karega	Hera Pheri	**Hey Ram!** (See p. 136)	Josh

1990

Director V. Shantaram, known for his film *Dr Kotnis ki Amar Kahani* (1946), dies.

(See p. 136)

Dilwale Dulhaniya Le Jayenge

Cast Shah Rukh Khan, Kajol, Amrish Puri, Farida Jalal, Anupam Kher
Director Aditya Chopra
Music Jatin, Lalit
Lyrics Anand Bakshi

One of Indian cinema's largest grossers, *Dilwale Dulhaniya Le Jayenge* made cinema rich in many ways. Not only did it give to the illustrious banner Yashraj Films a reason to rejoice resourcefully, it also provided Indian cinema with a new genre of entertainment. The Non-Resident Indian's experience came to the fore as Raj (Shah Rukh Khan) followed Simran (Kajol) from England to a village in Punjab to discover roots and romance. It was a heady combination of traditional values and universal emotions packaged in a cosmopolitan gloss that made the film a rage across the globe. Immensely clever, the film resorted to every formulaic convention to win the audience and yet did so with such endearing élan that audiences submitted to the sleek all-is-well message without a murmur of cynical protest. Jatin-Lalit's popular music score and Manmohan Singh's controlled but glamorous camera added their own allure to the NRI's search for a bride that takes him from Europe to Punjab. Love conquers all—but only after the audience has had its fill of courtship rituals and family protests.

TIMELINE: FILMS AND LANDMARK EVENTS

2000	**2000**	2000	**2000**	2000
Jungle	**Kabhi Khushi Kabhie Gham** (p 118)	Kahin Pyar Na Ho Jaye	**Kaho Na... Pyar Hai** (See p. 90)	Khauff

1990

Choli ke peeche kya hai from Subhash Ghai's *Saudagar* becomes the most controversial film song to date.

Hum Dil De Chuke Sanam 1999

Cast Salman Khan, Aishwarya Rai, Ajay Devgan, Vikram Gokhale, Smita Jayekar, Helen, Zohra Sehgal
Director Sanjay Leela Bhansali
Music Ismail Durbar
Lyrics Mehboob

With Anil Mehta's cinematography to support Sanjay Leela Bhansali's resplendent vision and his sister Bela Sehgal to cut the director's frames into a pastiche of elegant chic, *Hum Dil...* is a visual feast. Ismail Durbar's music score heightens the film's mood of mellow passion. The first half of the elegiac romance, set in a sprawling Gujarati mansion, builds a romance between the household's favourite daughter (Aishwarya Rai) and the rakish music student from Italy (Salman Khan). In the second half the hitherto chirpy Rai, married to a man she doesn't love, moves into a sultry silence as her noble husband (Ajay Devgan) decides to reunite her with her lover in Italy. It's a genre-defying romance that changed the narrative and mood patterns of love stories in Hindi cinema.

Watch out for directors Karan Johar and Arjun Sablok in *Dilwale Dulhaniya Le Jayenge* (1995), playing Shah Rukh's buddies during the decisive European tour when the rivers of romance flow and irrigate the remotest corners of Aditya Chopra's plot.

2000	2000	2000	2000	2000
Kurukshetra	Mela	Mission Kashmir	Mohabbatein	Phir Bhi Dil Hai Hindustani

1991

Cable and satellite television come to India following the Gulf War.

Na Tum Jano Na Hum

2002

Cast Hrithik Roshan, Esha Deol, Saif Ali Khan
Director Arjun Sablok
Music Rajesh Roshan
Lyrics Anand Bakshi

Every frame, gesture, nuance and twitch of this film conveys a rich array of romantic emotions. Every shot has a reason and every pause in the narrative takes us to a new plateau of elation. This film looks and feels like a dream. Arjun Sablok reveals a flair for fragile shot compositions. Vivid glimpses of rustling silk and whispering affections align the film's narrative structure. At the centre of Sablok's uniquely tender universe is a rather wispy triangle comprising two dreamers who belong to each other by the truest classical definition of love, and a realist who unknowingly comes between them. Esha (Esha Deol) is the incurable romantic who believes there's someone somewhere meant for her. Rahul (Hrithik Roshan) is a reticent, romantic photographer protective of and yet amused by his rich and privileged best friend Akshay's (Saif Ali Khan) philandering. The relationship between the rich and pampered Akshay and his family's 'adopted' son Rahul and the heartbreaking sacrifices that the quietly sensitive Rahul is expected to make,

echo the Amitabh Bachchan-Vinod Mehra friendship in Hrishikesh Mukherjee's *Bemisaal*. Hrithik Roshan gives the most brilliantly accomplished performance of his career, proving he has no equal among today's performing stars. His dancing, done sparingly for a change, is like a waltz of life. It astonishes how austerely Arjun Sablok uses Rajesh Roshan's melodious music when he has so much of it to give to us. It's like a man who saves up his riches for a rainy day.

TIMELINE: FILMS AND LANDMARK EVENTS

2000	2000	2000	2000	2000
Pukar (See p. 91)	Raja Ko Rani Se Pyar Ho Gaya	Raju Chacha	Refugee	Shikari

1991

Actress Nutan and director Raj Khosla pass away.

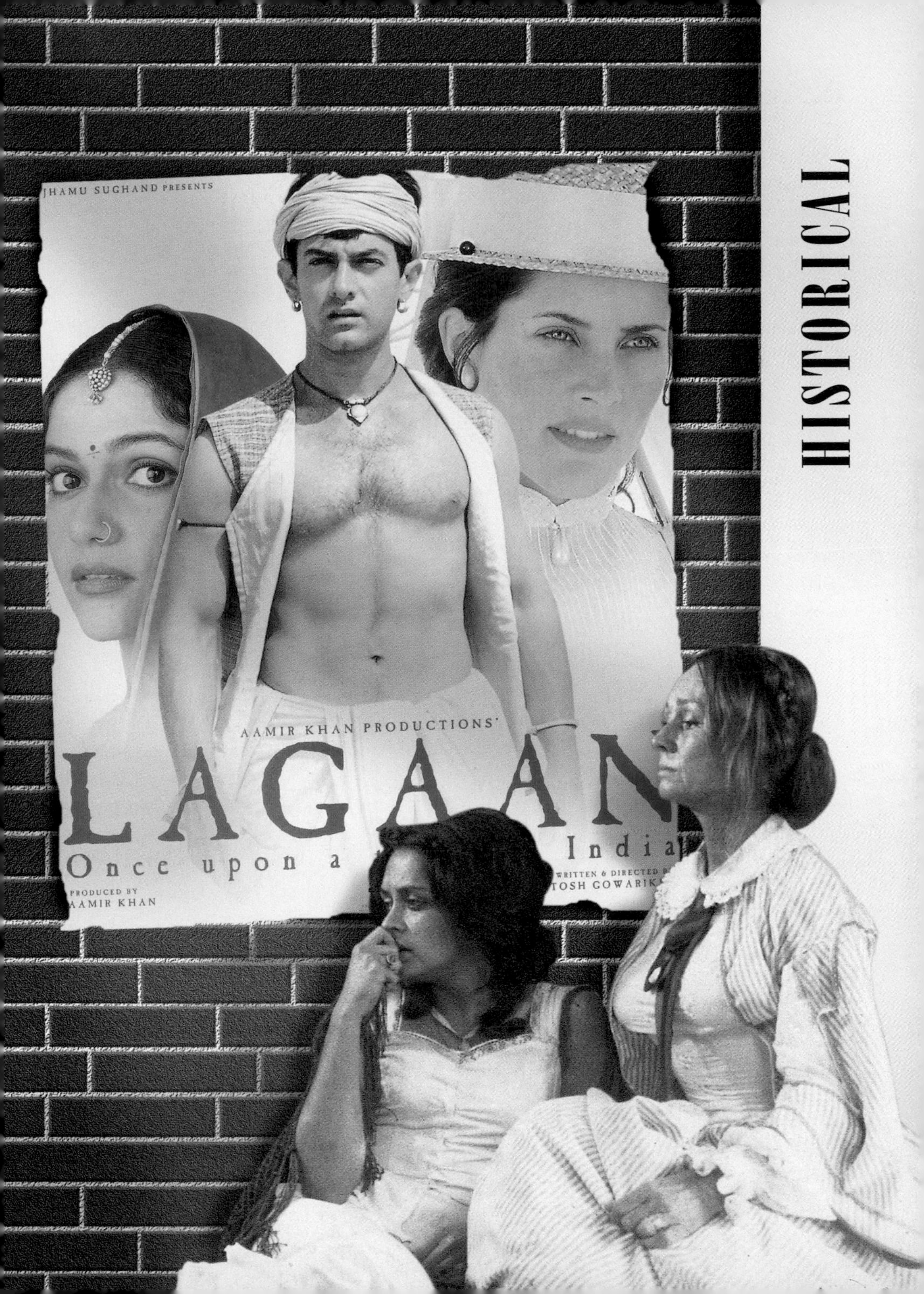
JHAMU SUGHAND PRESENTS
AAMIR KHAN PRODUCTIONS'
LAGAAN
Once upon a
India
PRODUCED BY
AAMIR KHAN

HISTORICAL

Junoon 1978

Cast Shashi Kapoor, Shabana Azmi, Nafisa Ali, Jennifer Kapoor, Naseeruddin Shah
Director Shyam Benegal
Music Vanraj Bhatia

An enchanting mix of myth and fact, *Junoon* brought to the screen a heated forbidden liaison between a mutinous Pathan (Shashi Kapoor) and a beauteous Britisher (Nafisa Ali). Director Shyam Benegal who had so far made intimate portraits of the fissures at the grassroots of Indian existence, swerved into the epic mode with fairly stunning results. With Govind Nihalani looking astutely through the camera lens, *Junoon* is the consummate peaen to periodicity with first-rate performances by all, from Shashi Kapoor's father-in-law Geoffrey Kendall to Shabana Azmi as his sultry Begum who seethes as his liaison with the British woman progresses. Based on Ruskin Bond's *A Flight Of Pigeons,* the film is a sanguine and highly passionate feast of emotions and visuals assembled with care.

Hey Ram! 2000

Cast Kamal Haasan, Rani Mukherjee, Vasundhara Das, Atul Kulkarni, Hema Malini, Naseeruddin Shah, Shah Rukh Khan
Director Kamal Haasan
Music Ilaiyaraja   **Lyrics** Sameer

Hey Ram brings to the screen a panoramic sweep and epic view of Indian history seldom seen in Indian cinema, portraying the journey of Saket Ram (Kamal Haasan) who travels from Tamil Nadu to Bengal to Delhi in search of a political and individual identity, only to realize that the demon he seeks to vanquish is within himself. In its Kafkaesque depiction of the sheer largesse and ambiguity of India's socio-political ethos, and in its treatment of fiction in a historical context, *Hey Ram* is an experiment with tooth and nail. Every portion of this tale is radiant with the poetry of politics.

TIMELINE: FILMS AND LANDMARK EVENTS

2000	2000	2000	2001	2001
Tera Jadoo Chal Gaya	Yaadein	Zubeidaa	Ajnabee	Aks

1992

The American Academy of Motion Picture Arts and Sciences awards Satyajit Ray an Oscar for lifetime achievement. He is also awarded the Bharat Ratna.

Asoka

2001

Cast Shah Rukh Khan, Kareena Kapoor, Danny Denzongpa, Rahul Dev, Hrishita Bhatt, Subhasini Ali

Director Santosh Sivan

Music Anu Malik

Lyrics Anand Bakshi, Gulzar

Santosh Sivan who had earlier made small but stunning films like the children's flick *Halo* and the treatise on terrorism *Terrorist*, leapt into the league of the luminous with a film that recreates the life, times and largely imaginary loves of the Mauryan king Asoka who renounced the throne and its thorny confusions for Buddhism. In the double capacity of director and cinematographer, Santosh Sivan blended the poetry of history into a 'mellow'-drama that made a terrific impact. The film has wonderful sequences of war that actually condemn bloodshed rather than romanticize it. Especially vivid are scenes in the climactic battle where unbearable pain is written on Asoka's face as he sees the remnants of the ravages of man fighting man (and woman, as Shah Rukh takes on Kareena!) for territorial supremacy. Wonderful images of primeval passion underscore the main love story between Asoka and the untameable Princess Kaurawki (Kareena Kapoor in a startling performance). The film features interesting cameos from director Umesh Mehra (playing Asoka's father) and politician Subhasini Ali (as Asoka's mother).

Lagaan (2001) ushered Bollywood into the international cinema scene with a velocity last felt when Satyajit Ray and Bimal Roy put forward their famine fables *Pather Panchali* (in Bengali) and *Do Bigha Zameen* (in Hindi). Coincidentally, *Lagaan*, Gowariker's big breakthrough hit was also about a famine and its unexpected aftermath.

2001	2001	**2001**	2001	**2001**
Asoka	Bas Itna Sa Khwaab	**Chandni Bar**	Deham	**Dil Chahta Hai**
(See p. 137)	Hai	(See p. 92)		(See p. 92)

1992

Prolific director Satyajit Ray, one of the most influential presences in Indian cinema, passes away.

Lagaan

2001

Cast Aamir Khan, Gracy Singh, Rachel Shelley, Paul Blackthorne
Director Ashutosh Gowarikar
Music A.R. Rahman
Lyrics Javed Akhtar

An inspirational fairytale about a bunch of peasants taking on their colonial oppressors during the British rule in India. A dhoti-clad and crew-cut Khan pulls off the extraordinarily heroic character of Bhuvan who leads his villagers to a sporty victory. Cleverly plotted, the long climactic sequence—almost 45 minutes—consists of a rabble-rousing cricket match between the oppressed colonists and the arrogant colonizers. It makes the narrative crackle with a contemporary energy generally absent in period films. Set in 1893, the film's ensemble cast, helmed by producer Aamir Khan, adds an effortless epic lustre to the tale. The love triangle between Bhuvan, the wide-eyed village belle Gauri (Gracy Singh) and the British Memsahib Elizabeth (Rachel Shelley) worked with a lubricated luminosity. Cinematographer Anil Mehta, art director Nitin Chandrakant Desai and costume designer Bhanu Athaiya do a creative ménage-a-trois. *Lagaan* looks and feels wonderfully alive and vibrant. The toasted-brown outdoors of the Bhuj district in Gujarat are teased into a tremulous authenticity by A.R. Rahman's skilled music and songs which weave in and out of the striking pastiche of nostalgia, patriotism and the competitive spirit. This is one of the most important and influential Hindi films of modern times. Deftly straddling both romance and sports, *Lagaan* is a painting with the canvas sprayed in colours that are no slave to time.

TIMELINE: FILMS AND LANDMARK EVENTS

2001	2001	2001	2001	2001
Ehsaas	Ek Rishta	Filhaal	Gadar: Ek Prem Katha	Ishq Vishq Pyaar Vyaar

1992

Shah Rukh Khan erupts on screen in Raj Kanwar's *Deewana*.

ACTION

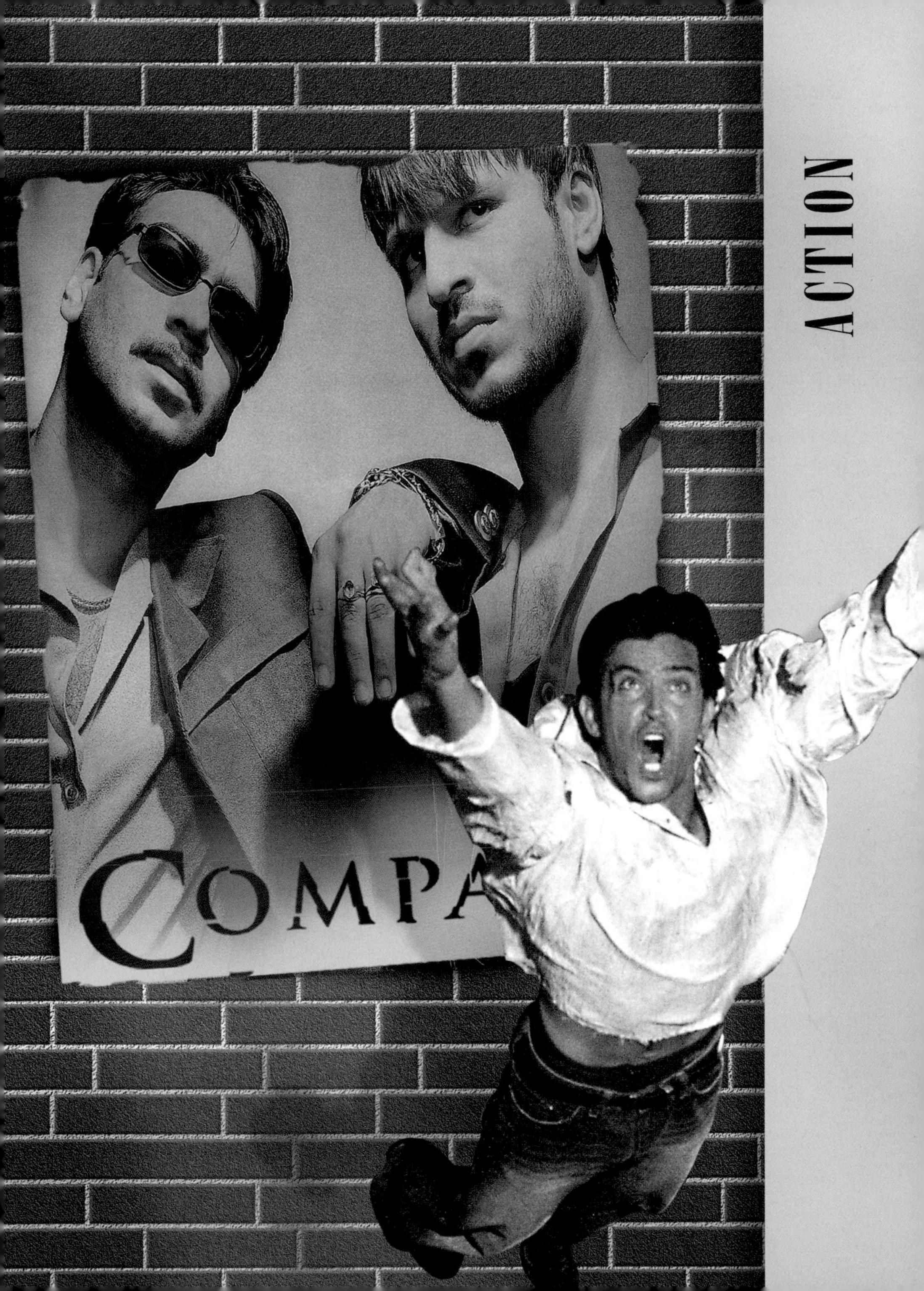

Dacait

1987

Cast Raakhee, Sunny Deol, Meenakshi Sheshadri, Paresh Rawal

Director Rahul Rawail

Music R.D. Burman

Lyrics Javed Akhtar

*D*acait takes us into the ravines of Chambal Valley to show the class persecution of Deol's character and his family to the extent that he becomes an outlaw. Rawail's treatment of the dacoit drama is singularly striking. Never before have the crust-brown deserts and the parched-yellow ravines looked so threatening and symbolic of the persecutions of the downtrodden. There are harrowing moments of violence, more damning for their emotional than physical impact. The implosive impact of Deol's performance was complemented by Paresh Rawal's portrayal of the loutish law-defying cop who is as unscrupulous as he is avaricious. *Dacait* painted a landscape of abject desolation and despair. ◀

Hathyar

1989

Cast Dharmendra, Rishi Kapoor, Sanjay Dutt, Amrita Singh, Kulbhushan Kharbanda, Asha Parekh, Sangeeta Bijalani, Paresh Rawal

Director J.P. Dutta

Lyrics Hassan Kamal

*H*athyar did a remarkable job of portraying the end of innocence and the beginning of crime in the life of its protagonist Sanjay Dutt who moves to Mumbai with his innocent parents (Asha Parekh, in one of her last screen appearances; and J.P. Dutta's favourite actor, Kulbhushan Kharbanda). Once in the city Dutt gets sucked into a world of crime, represented in the film by two kinds of outcasts, the benign don played by Dharmendra and the low-down gangster Paresh Rawal. Sanjay Dutt, in his career's best, goes from vulnerability to violence sometimes bringing both qualities into the same range of vision.

TIMELINE: FILMS AND LANDMARK EVENTS

2001	2001	2001	2001	2001
Lagaan	Lajja	Love Ke Liye Kuch Bhi Karega	Love You Hamesha	Mujhe Kuch Kehna Hai

1992

Amjad Khan, the dreaded Gabbar Singh of Ramesh Sippy's *Sholay* (1975), passes away.

Ghayal

Cast Sunny Deol, Meenakshi Sheshadri, Raj Babbar, Moushumi Chatterjee, Amrish Puri

Director Raj Kumar Santoshi

Music Bappi Lahiri

Lyrics Anjaan, Indivar

A revenge saga with a difference. Raj Kumar Santoshi's blood-splattered debut showed him to be a craftsman of unforeseen devices. Though *Ghayal* is a routine revenge drama, the entire framing of the narrative and the editing pattern are so unique as to give the plot a look of innovative bravado. Sunny Deol, controlled and sinewy as a man seeking revenge on his brother's killers is in splendid shape. The taut plot trotted forward and at a breakneck though even speed culminating in an unexpected climax. More than the narrative it was the way Santoshi told the age-old story which made it many cuts above the rut. *Ghayal* was designed by Sunny Deol's production house as a vehicle to exploit his image as the strong and silent hero. It was a smash hit and clearly indicated where the future of mainstream Hindi cinema lay.

Apart from focussing the narrative's energy almost entirely on the action sequences, Santoshi's film *Ghayal* (1990) also began the process in mainstream Hindi cinema of sidelining the music to concentrate on the plot in the drama. The violence overtakes the violins in this gritty action film.

1994

The 'first lady' of the Indian screen, actress Devika Rani, passes away.

Company 2002

Cast Ajay Devgan, Manisha Koirala,
Antara Mali, Mohan Lal, Seema
Biswas, Vivek Oberoi
Director Ram Gopal Varma
Music Sandeep Chowta
Lyrics N. Raikwat, T. Romani, J. Sahni

Never before has a Hindi film on crime and punishment achieved such an extraordinary synthesis of violence and poetry—an underworld film of such exceptional resonances that takes us deep into the heart and mind of organized crime. The film achieves a sense of completeness of no other film by Ram Gopal Varma. Malik (Ajay Devgan) is the silently seething gangster who immediately takes on the volatile street hoodlum Chandu (Vivek Oberoi) under his wings. The sound design, the lighting of faces and frame, the exotic locations (which are used not as tantalizing visuals but authentic characters), Sandeep Chowta's extraordinarily expressive and assertive background music and above all, debutant cinematographer Hemant Chaturvedi's skills behind the camera come together to lend a luminous epic quality to the main text and subtle subtexts which run across this tactile tale of terrible tensions.

TIMELINE: FILMS AND LANDMARK EVENTS

2002	2002	2002	**2002**	2002
Aankhen	Agni Varsha	Awara Paagal Deewana	**Company** (See p. 142)	Deewangee

1994

Manmohan Desai, who directed many films, including *Amar Akbar Anthony* (1977), passes away.

BLAZE
FILM ENTERPRISES
PVT. LTD. PRESENTS

Bhumika
EASTMANCOLOR
(THE ROLE)

Produced by : LALIT M. BIJLANI · FRENI M. VARIAVA

Starring :

SMITA PATIL · ANANT NAG
AMRISH PURI · NASEERUDDIN SHAH
SULABHA DESHPANDE
KULBHUSHAN KHARBANDA
BABY RUKHSANA · B.V. KAR
and AMOL PALEKA

Music :VANRAJ BHATIA
Screenplay : GIRISH KARNAD
SATYA DEV DUBEY and SHYAM BENEGAL
Dialogue: PT. SATYA DEV DUBEY
Photography :GOVIND NIHALANI

Direction :
SHYAM BENEGAL

PARALLEL CINEMA

Ankur
1973

Cast Shabana Azmi, Anant Nag, Sadhu Meher
Director (and Screenplay) Shyam Benegal
Music Salil Chowdhury
Lyrics Yogesh

Benegal, who came to this film after numerous ads to his credit, conceived *Ankur* as an avant-garde neo-realistic film. It ushered in a new wave of realism in Indian cinema. Shabana Azmi, playing the adultress wife of a physically challenged labourer (Sadhu Meher) blows the screen apart in her climactic tirade where she lashes out at her landlord lover (Anant Nag) and by proxy, at the whole system of caste oppression that still governs many areas of our country. Govind Nihalani's camera captured the Hyderabadi ruralscape as a mute spectator to the stunning saga of socio-sexual exploitation that unfolded in the foreground. *Ankur* revels in the resonances of tyranny.

Rajnigandha
1973

Cast Amol Palekar, Vidya Sinha, Dinesh Thakur
Director Basu Chatterjee
Music Salil Chowdhury
Lyrics Yogesh

Rajnigandha is considered a breakthrough film for the arthouse cinema. Released the same year as *Ankur*, both films made profits at

the box office and are rightly lauded for changing the fate of small-budgeted independent films free of formulistic motives. This is a working-class romance about a girl (Vidya Sinha) with two men in her life. In his first foray in films Palekar won a special status among Bollywood actors for representing the face of the ordinary man. Chatterjee moves through buses and local trains in the melee of Mumbai creating a counterpoint to the studio-made films that prevailed in Hindi cinema.

TIMELINE: FILMS AND LANDMARK EVENTS

2002	2002	2002	2002	2002
Devdas	Ek Chotisi Prem	Na Tum Jano Na	Khushi	Mere Yaar Ki Shaadi
(See p. 93)	Kahani	Hum		

1994

Music composer R.D. Burman, son of S.D. Burman, passes away. R.D. Burman was known for his music in films like *Caravan* (1971), and *Hare Rama, Hare Krishna* (1972).

Bhumika

1977

Cast Smita Patil, Amol Palekar, Anant Nag, Amrish Puri, Naseeruddin Shah
Director Shyam Benegal
Music Vanraj Bhatia
Lyrics Ajit Varman

Bhumika is a film about the mask of hypocrisy that the male wears when it comes to dealing with the other sex, ultimately bringing the rebellious actress' life to a full and self defeating circle. Smita Patil's best-known film casts her as Usha, a character based on Hansa Wadkar, a Marathi actress of the 1940s. Faintly fictionalized, Usha's emotional insecurities guide her through a maze of eccentric male gaze, making her wilt, piece by piece. The film's evocation of the period gone by is slight but effective.

Ankur (1973) Shyam Benegal's revolutionary debut as a feature filmmaker is wrongly considered to be Shabana's maiden appearance. In fact she did another film, K.A Abbas's *Faasla* (1974), before sauntering to Benegal's maiden feature film. The role of Laxmi was offered to many other actresses including Waheeda Rehman, the Andhraite actress Sharda, Aparna Sen and even Anju Mahendroo.

2002	2002	2002	2002	2002
Mitr—My Friend	Om Jai Jagdish	Pitaah	Raaz	Road

1995
Marks the centenary of world cinema.

Nishant

1978

Cast Girish Karnad, Shabana Azmi, Anant Nag,
Amrish Puri, Smita Patil, Naseeruddin Shah
Director Shyam Benegal
Music Vanraj Bhatia   **Lyrics** Mohammed Qutb Shah

*N*ishant tells the story of a schoolteacher (Girish Karnad) whose wife (Shabana Azmi) is kidnapped and raped by a clan of feudal landlords. The teacher's poignant fight for justice forms the crux of this hard-hitting drama, lifted to classical heights by the performers. Smita Patil and Naseeruddin Shah in their first major appearances blew the screen apart with their smouldering intensity. The savagely violent mood puts this work outside the purview of the squeamish. *Nishant* inspired a succession of films on oppression.

Ek Bar Phir

1979

Cast Deepti Naval, Suresh Oberoi, Pradeep Verma
Director Vinod Pande
Music Raghunath Seth

*V*inod Pande's experiment with marital truth was made on a shoestring budget with three newcomers. Naval, demure and sensitive was perfectly cast opposite the brash and insensitive character played by Suresh Oberoi. He was the perfect alibi for an impulsive fling with a roadside painter Pradeep Verma (who disappeared from cinema after his debut). Unusually enough, the wife 'dared' to sleep with her lover and also decided to leave her husband at the end for a happier life. The bold anti-conventional treatment caught the viewers' fancy and *Ek Bar Phir* was quite a cult success.

TIMELINE: FILMS AND LANDMARK EVENTS

2002	2002	2002	2003	2003
Saathiya	Samay	The Legend of Bhagat Singh	Baghban	Bhoot

1995

Dilip Kumar is awarded the Dadasaheb Phalke Award for his contribution to the Indian film industry.

Aakrosh

Cast Om Puri, Naseeruddin Shah, Smita Patil, Amrish Puri
Director Govind Nihalani
Music Ajit Varman

From the eerie preamble to the stunning finale (a jolting end eventually became a trademark of Nihalani's stark and dark cinema) *Aakrosh* takes us into a warped world of brutal oppression. Om Puri as the speechless victim of oppression accused of murdering his own wife (Smita Patil, in a smouldering cameo) is a force to reckon with. As his defence lawyer, Naseeruddin Shah was effectively underplayed. His search for the truth behind the tribal's terrifying silence provided the playwright Vijay Tendulkar's screenplay with a canny combination of social purpose and cinematic thrills. Though *Aakrosh* is based on a true incident it never sacrifices cinematic purity to the trendy documentary element. This is a film about smothered screams and screaming silences.

Naseeruddin Shah's love for acting began in school. After studying at the National School of Drama in Delhi, he was discovered by director Shyam Benegal and cast in *Nishant* (1978). He very soon became Benegal's favourite actor and was given several more roles in his films.

2003	2003	2003	2003	2003
Boom	Chameli	Darna Mana Hai	Dil Ka Rishta	Janasheen

1996

Actress Nadia of *Hunterwali* (1935) fame passes away.

Chakra   1981

Cast Smita Patil, Naseeruddin Shah,
    Ranjit Chowdhary
Director Rabindra Dharmaraj
Music Hridayanath Mangeshkar

The director, who died soon after making the film, extracted a National Award winning performance from Smita Patil. Patil plays a migrant slum-dweller in Mumbai eking out a livelihood with her son (Ranjit Chowdhary) The story that follows is a dark tale of brutal poverty and deprivation. Naseeruddin Shah puts in an interesting supporting role as a pimp. An interesting music score by the grossly underrated Hridayanath Mangeshkar adds to the films earthy lustre.

Subah   1981

Cast Smita Patil, Girish Karnad
Director Jabbar Patel
Music Hridayanath Mangeshkar
Lyrics Suresh Bhatt, Vasant Bapat

Asserting Smita Patil's powerful feminist presence this Hindi-Marathi bi-lingual (*Umbartha* in Marathi) delineates the real-life story of Sulabha (Patil) a housewife who steps out of her spousal cocoon to challenge corrupt practices in an institute for destitute women. Once in the thick of the corruption, Patil's character undergoes many life-changing experiences that bring her close to her own search for an identity. *Subah* is remarkable predominantly for Patil's performance and the conclusion where the husband refuses to take her back after she returns home from her mission. Director Jabbar Patel's strong roots in Marathi culture and folk theatre afforded him a view into the workings of Maharashtrian culture and politics.

TIMELINE: FILMS AND LANDMARK EVENTS

2003	2003	2003	2003	2003
Jhankaar Beats	Jism	Joggers Park	Kaante	Kal Ho Na Ho

1996
Legendary actor Raj Kumar dies.

Bazaar

Cast Smita Patil, Naseeruddin Shah, Supriya Pathak, Farooq Shaikh
Director Sagar Sarhadi
Music Khayyam
Lyrics Mir Taqi Mir, Makhdoon Mohiuddin

A low-budget semi-experimental film telling an acutely poignant tale of a young Muslim girl's brutally mismatched marriage to a Gulf

sheikh, *Bazaar* was a film with a gaping social conscience. Smita Patil agrees to find a nubile Hyderabadi bride for her lover's (Bharat Kapoor) rich friend because he has promised to marry her in return. A beautiful blend of drama and social commentary, *Bazaar* is buoyed by the brilliant ensemble cast. The other outstanding component in this drama of exploitation is Khayyam's music score.

Lata Mangeshkar regards *Dikhayi diye yun ke bekhud kiya* in *Bazaar* (1982) as one of her best songs ever. Very few realistic dramas have merged the poetry and politics of an issue-based drama so brilliantly with music. Sagar Sarhadi never released another film, though he did direct one more, unreleased, film *Tere Shaher Mein* again with Smita Patil in the lead and Khayyam's music.

2003	2003	**2003**	2003	2003
Khakee	Khwahish	**Koi... Mil Gaya** (See p. 94)	Kuch Naa Kaho	Main Madhuri Dixit Banna Chahti Hoon

2001

Ashutosh Gowariker's *Lagaan* is nominated for an Oscar in the Best Foreign Film category.

Arth

1983

Cast Shabana Azmi, Kulbhushan Kharbanda, Smita Patil, Rohini Hattangadi, Raj Kiran
Director Mahesh Bhatt
Music Jagjit Singh
Lyrics Kaifi Azmi

This marital drama about a deserted wife's quest for self assertion is to this day regarded as a genre-defining, probing and piercing tale of redemptive emotions that spill out with volcanic force. Azmi's performance in *Arth* can be calibrated according to the moments that Bhatt's script afforded her hefty histrionic sequences. Shabana Azmi provides us with a deeply empathetic feminist statement.

Arth remains a testimony to the raw velocity that Bhatt exercised over his footage.

Bhavna

1984

Cast Shabana Azmi, Marc Zuber, Master Makharand, Saeed Jaffrey
Director Pravin Bhatt
Music Bappi Lahiri
Lyrics Kaifi Azmi

Bhavna is a tempestuous tale of an abandoned woman's struggle to bring up her child with dignity and luxury. In the course of this beautifully mounted drama Azmi goes from a starry-eyed idealistic woman to a conned and cornered wife and finally to a determined mother who turns to prostitution to fulfill her dreams of making her son a doctor. Cinematographer Pravin Bhatt's directorial debut was a devastating portrait of a mother and child done in the golden colours of love and honour.

TIMELINE: FILMS AND LANDMARK EVENTS

2003	2003	2003	2003	2003
Makdee	Maqbool	Mujhe Kuch Kehna Hai	Mumbai Matinee	Munnabhai MBBS

2001

Ashok Kumar, legendary actor of films such as *Acchut Kanya* (1936) and *Kismet* (1943) passes away.

Paroma

1984

Cast Raakhee, Rahul Sharma, Dipankar De, Anil Chatterjee, Aparna Sen
Director Aparna Sen
Music Bhaskar Chandavarkar
Lyrics Gulzar

Raakhee in her most powerful performance played a middle-aged, bored Bengali housewife who drifts into a scandalous love affair with an Non-Resident Indian fashion photographer (played by director Sen's husband Rahul Sharma). The film's explicit view of sexual and emotional dereliction sparked off debates on middle-class morality. There are several audaciously unconventional sequences such as the one where Paroma lies inert under her husband humming a song absent-mindedly during the sex act. There's also the suggestion of a kiss between the housewife and her lover that raised the hackles of moralists. But beyond all the shock value provided by the script there is a sensitive story of a woman's need to break away from the various socially sanctioned roles in life. Raakhee was splendidly in character. The director Aparna Sen played a cameo as the leading lady's friend. Ashok Mehta's camerawork rooted the lead character to Bengal while making her a woman in search of answers to questions on her monotonous existence.

Morbid and mordant sequences between the errant husband (an underplayed Kharbanda in his only starring role ever!) and his neurotic mistress (Smita Patil) in *Arth* (1983) were allegedly taken from director Mahesh Bhatt's own stormy relationship with actress Parveen Babi.

2003	2003	2003	**2003**	2003
Paap	Pinjar	Rules: Pyar Ka Superhit Formula	**Teen Deewarein** (See p. 158)	Tere Naam

2001
'India's Nightingale' Lata Mangeshkar receives the Bharat Ratna.

Saaransh

1984

Cast Anupam Kher, Rohini Hattangadi, Soni Razdan, Madan Jain, Nilu Phule
Director Mahesh Bhatt
Music Ajit Varman   **Lyrics** Vasant Dev

In his debut performance Anupam Kher played a man twice his age grappling with the loss of his only son in a freak accident. Bhatt's film posed serious questions on the meaning of death and the final futility of life. It did so while telling an inherently poignant story of a couple's efforts to protect a single girl (Soni Razdan) from the wrath of her boyfriend's politician-father (Nilu Phule). Scenes such as the one where the old protagonist battles red tape at the airport to get the ashes of his dead son are quoted as examples of the finest filmmaking in the country. Many believe this to be the best film Bhatt ever made, and there's little reason to doubt that. Incidentally the film's producer Rajshri wanted Sanjeev Kumar to play the protagonist. Director Bhatt fought to have only Kher play one of the rare protagonists who's above the age of 60 in Indian cinema.

Sparsh

1984

Cast Naseeruddin Shah, Shabana Azmi, Om Puri
Director Sai Paranjpye
Music Kanu Roy
Lyrics Indu Jain

A neo-realistic drama, justly lauded for its authentic depiction of the life of the blind, *Sparsh* is the tale of a blind man (Naseeruddin Shah) whose self-worth won't let him clutch at the loving hand of a widow (Shabana Azmi). Paranjpye shot the film on location in a blind school enhancing the authenticity of the film. Though rather lengthy and polemical, the relationship between the protagonists is given enough room to breathe and grow. *Sparsh* was

the most credible portrayal of the physically handicapped before Sanjay Leela Bhansali's *Khamoshi: The Musical* and *Black*.

TIMELINE: FILMS AND LANDMARK EVENTS

2004	2004	2004	2004	2004
Ab Tak Chhapan	Aitraaz	Charas	Dhoom	Ek Hasina Thi

2001

Actor Dev Anand is awarded the Padma Bhushan for his contribution to Indian cinema.

Ankush

1985

Cast Nana Patekar, Madan Jain, Arjun Chakraborty, Suhas
Palsikar, Nisha Singh
Director N. Chandra
Music Kuldeep Singh

In *Ankush*, Chandra exuded the raw energy of a truly individualistic creator. The savage street-level drama unfolds the story of four jobless men (Patekar, Jain, Palsikar and Chakraborty) whose friendship with the sweet and gentle girl-next-door (Nisha Singh) changes their lives. On the verge of starting a career the foursome suddenly swerve into crime when the girl they love is gang-raped. The tragedy transforms their will to conform into a social pattern and brands them as convicts and outcasts. The actors in *Ankush*, all new to cinema, lent a certain spiked edge to the entertainment-value of this socially conscious film. The fresh gaunt faces helped to imbue an imminent intuitiveness to the tale.

After *Ankush* (1985), Nana Patekar went on to become a major figure in Bollywood. He collaborated with director N.Chandra for two other films, the successful *Pratighaat* (1987) and the failure *Wajood* (1998).

2004	2004	2004	2004	2004
Gayab	Girlfriend	Hul Chal	Hum Tum	Krishna Cottage

2002

Sanjay Leela Bhansali's *Devdas* is screened at the Cannes Film Festival.

Mirch Masala 1985

Cast Smita Patil, Naseeruddin Shah, Om Puri, Deepti
       Naval, Dina Pathak, Supriya Pathak, Raj Babbar
Director Ketan Mehta
Music Rajat Dholakia   Lyrics Babubhai Ranpura

The versatile Ketan Mehta's most celebrated film is a work of flamboyance and artistry. A a parable on male oppression, *Mirch Masala* features Smita Patil in one of her several strongly underscored feminist parts, as the free-spirited and rebellious Sonbai. When threatened with abduction by the village subedar (Naseeruddin Shah) she seeks shelter in a red chilli factory. Most of the film's effulgent images centre on the shades of red chilli as complemented by the clothes and demeanour of the women in the factory.

Paar 1985

Cast Naseeruddin Shah, Shabana Azmi
Director Gautam Ghose

A parable of exploitation photographed fetchingly by the director himself, *Paar* traverses the wretched lives of two peasants Naurangia (Naseeruddin Shah) and his wife Rama (Shabana Azmi) who, in an effort to purge their lives of dereliction and homelessness, take a herd of pigs across a fast-flowing river for a measly sum of money. The film works as both a metaphor and an adventure story. The actors, at great risk, undertook the crucial crossing of the river. The authenticity of the milieu and the principal actors' conviction are projected into the plot imbuing it with a neo-realism echoing Satyajit Ray's Bengali masterpiece *Pather Panchali* thirty years earlier.

TIMELINE: FILMS AND LANDMARK EVENTS

2004	2004	2004	2004	2004
Kyon... Ho Gaya Na	Lakshya	Main Hoon Na	Masti	Mujhse Shaadi Karogi

2004

Actress Suraiya, an icon for her film roles during the 1940s—*Pyaar Ki Jeet* (1948) and *Dillagi* (1949)—dies at the age of 75.

Ek Pal

Cast Shabana Azmi, Naseeruddin Shah, Farooq Shaikh
Director Kalpana Lajmi
Music Bhupen Hazarika
Lyrics Gulzar

In her remarkable debut, Lajmi legitimized her antecedents as Guru Dutt's niece. This sentimental odyssey into the womb of a desolate woman was buoyed by several extraneous attention-grabbers: the exotic green Assam locales, for instance. Cinematographer K.K. Mahajan captured the great open spaces with lingering warmth that replicated the protagonist Priyam's (Azmi) unquenchable thirst to go from here to maternity. Priyam finally marries the sober and staid Naseeruddin Shah who cannot give her what she wants the most: a baby. An adulterous liaison with her ex-flame gives Priyam what she is looking for. Bhupen Hazarika's music is a stirring mix of Assamese folk and melodies that have a universal resonance.

There are dishy performances in *Mirch Masala* (1985) including two generations of the Pathak women, mom Dina and daughters Ratna and Supriya. But the real star of the show, besides Smita Patil, is Jehangir Chowdhury's cinematography that whips up peppery poetry out of a simple parable of oppression and protest.

2004	2004	2004	2004	2004
Murder	Naach	Padmashree Laloo Prasad Yadav	Plan	Raincoat

2004

Actor Mehmood, well known for his comic roles in films like *Dil Tera Deewana* (1962) and *Padosan* (1968) among many others, passes away.

Bandit Queen 1994

Cast Seema Biswas, Nirmal Pandey, Manoj Bajpai, Govind Namdeo

Director Shekhar Kapur

Music Nusrat Fateh Ali Khan

Lyrics Nusrat Fateh Ali Khan, M. Arshad

Based on the life of the dacoit Phoolan Devi, *Bandit Queen* is a harrowing exposition on the life of some women at the grassroot levels. Kapur's journey into the heart of darkness begins when, as a child, Phoolan is married off. The portrait of savage brutality continues, reaching a crescendo in Phoolan's gang-rape by the Thakurs who troop in one by one for three days to ravage Phoolan. To no one's surprise, she takes to the gun. Her dacoity is filmed with a combination of cinematic splendour and documentary authenticity. Its vision of a stark landscape matches the total desolation of the characters. The brutal language in the dialogues by Ranjit Kapoor convey a steep amount of intimacy and immediacy in the interaction between the protagonist and her adversaries who begin to attack her from her childhood.

◄

Hazaar Chaurasi Ki Maa 1997

Cast Jaya Bachchan, Anupam Kher, Joy Sengupta, Seema Biswas, Nandita Das

Director Govind Nihalani

Music Debajyoti Mishra

Jaya Bachchan's magnificent comeback after seventeen years, portraying litterateur Mahashweta Devi's heroine Sujata Chatterjee. Sujata's middle-class Kolkatan life is shattered one night by the shrill ringing of the phone informing her to come and inspect her son's corpse in the city morgue. Thus begins Sujata's journey into her own life as well as her son's, about a world she discovers only after her own is shattered. Bachchan's two lengthy sequences with Seema Biswas (an impoverished woman also grieving for her dead son) and Nandita Das (the dead son's girlfriend) are passionately executed. Nihalani spares us none of the brutal violence that marked the systematic annihilation of all young Naxalites shedding blood for a better social order in Bengal during the 1970s.

TIMELINE: FILMS AND LANDMARK EVENTS

2004	2004	2004	2004	**2004**
Shabd	Swades	Tumsa Nahin Dekha	Vaastu Shastra	**Yuva**
				(See p. 95)

2005

Actress Nirupa Roy, screen mother to Amitabh Bachchan in a string of blockbusters during the 1970s and '80s, passes away.

Cast Tabu, Sachin Khadekar, Mohnish Behl, Namrata Shirodkar, Smita Jaykar
Director Mahesh Manjrekar
Music Rahul Ranade, Sukhwinder Singh
Lyrics Shrirang Godbole

A path-breaking performance by Tabu as a repressed middle-class Maharashtrian wife who's given the boot by her husband and son after a sexual transgression from the past comes tumbling out, gave a certainly opulent odour to this disturbing marital drama. Like Shabana Azmi in *Arth* and Smita Patil in *Subah*, Tabu questioned the entire ethos of middle-class marriages, the hypocrisy of a patriarchal society where men can get away with flings but women are not allowed the chance to even plead their case after a sexual aberration. The film moves through a series of conflicting emotions from repression to anguish to tentative defiance.

Perhaps one of the most versatile actors in Bollywood is Anupam Kher. With more than 200 films in his kitty, Kher juggles his act between commercial films, parallel cinema and crossover films with aplomb. He has won the Filmfare Award eight times and was awarded the Padma Shri by the Indian Government in 2004.

2005	**2005**	2005	2005	2005
Bewafa	**Black** (See p. 96)	Bunty Aur Babli	Kaal	Kisna

2005

Director Vijay Anand, who directed the hit film *Guide* (1965) passes away.

Teen Deewarein

2003

Cast Naseeruddin Shah, Jackie Shroff, Juhi Chawla, Nagesh Kukunoor, Gulshan Grover

Director Nagesh Kukunoor

Music Salim, Suleiman

Once in a while Indian cinema surprises you with its enterprising spirit. Nagesh Kukunoor's much talked-about prison drama is everything that you would expect—hard-hitting, gritty, absorbing, real and raw—and more. The finale is so imposingly conceived you want to salute the director for simply taking the initiative of stretching the outer limits of mass-oriented entertainment. Kukunoor touches upon the theme of capital punishment without really making a central issue of the matter. His three heroes Ishaan (Shah), Jaggu (Shroff) and Nagya (Kukunoor) are on death row. More than their impending end it's their life that interests Kukunoor. Having got satirical laughter out of himself, and us, in *Hyderabad Blues* and *Bollywood Calling*, Kukunoor now spreads his discernably strong vision of human caprice and destiny's damning jokes, across a theme of great power. As the Florence Nightingale who isn't as frail and powerless as she seems initially, Juhi Chawla makes you wonder where she's been holding in that immense sensitivity and depth.

TIMELINE: FILMS AND LANDMARK EVENTS

2005	2005	2005	2005	2005
Naina	Paheli	Socha Na Tha	Veer Zaara	Waqt

2005

Amrish Puri who immortalized the villain Mogambo in Shekhar Kapur's *Mr India* (1987) passes away.

YASH JOHAR PRESENTS DHARMA PRODUCTION'S

Kabhi Khushi
Kabhie Gham...

" Its all about loving your parents"   KARAN J

Top Actors

Heroes

1 Dilip Kumar
2 Raj Kapoor
3 Dev Anand
4 Pradeep Kumar
5 Bharat Bhushan

Heroines

1 Meena Kumari
2 Nargis
3 Madhubala
4 Geeta Bali
5 Vyjanthimala

Top 10 Hits

	Movie	Director	Cast
1	Babul	S.U. Sunny	Dilip Kumar, Nargis
2	Awara	Raj Kapoor	Raj Kapoor, Nargis, Prithiviraj Kapoor
3	Albela	Bhagwan	Bhagwan, Geeta Bali
4	Baiju Bawra	Vijay Bhatt	Bharat Bhushan, Meena Kumari
5	Anarkali	Nandalal Jaswantlal	Bina Rai, Pradeep Kumar
6	Nagin	Nandalal Jaswantlal	Pradeep Kumar, Vyjanthimala
7	Shri 420	Raj Kapoor	Raj Kapoor, Nargis, Nadira
8	Mother India	Mehboob Khan	Raj Kumar, Nargis, Sunil Dutt, Rajendra Kumar
9	Naya Daur	B.R. Chopra	Dilip Kumar, Vyjanthimala
10	Madhumati	Bimal Roy	Dilip Kumar, Vyjanthimala

Top 10 Flops

	Movie	Director	Cast
1	Jogan	Kidar Sharma	Nargis, Dilip Kumar
2	Aan	Mehboob Khan	Nimmi, Dilip Kumar, Nadira
3	Daera	Kamal Amrohi	Meena Kumar, Nasir Khan
4	Footpath	Zia Sarhadi	Meena Kumari, Dilip Kumar
5	Boot Polish	Prakash Arora	Baby Naaz, Rattan Kumar
6	Insaniyat	S.S. Vasan	Dilip Kumar, Dev Anand, Bina Rai
7	Jagte Raho	Sombhu Mitra	Raj Kapoor, Motilal
8	Musafir	Hrishikesh Mukherjee	Suchitra Sen, Dilip Kumar, Kishore Kumar
9	Phir Subah Hogi	Ramesh Saigal	Raj Kapoor, Mala Sinha
10	Kaagaz Ke Phool	Guru Dutt	Guru Dutt, Waheeda Rehman

Left: Dilip Kumar and Vyjanthimala in *Madhumati*.

Right: Guru Dutt and Mala Sinha in *Pyaasa*.

Facing page: Raj Kapoor and Nargis in *Awara*.

1960s

Top 10 Hits

	Movie	Director	Cast
1	Ganga Jumna	Nitin Bose	Dilip Kumar, Vyjanthimala, Nasir Khan
2	Junglee	Subodh Mukherjee	Shammi Kapoor, Saira Banu
3	Mere Mehboob	H.S . Rawail	Ashok Kumar, Rajendra Kumar, Sadhana
4	Padosan	Jyoti Swarup	Sunil Dutt ,Saira Banu, Kishore Kumar, Mehmood
5	Dosti	Satyen Bose	Sudhir Kumar, Sushil Kumar
6	Sangam	Raj Kapoor	Raj Kapoor, Vyjanthimala, Rajendra Kumar
7	Guide	Vijay Anand	Dev Anand, Waheeda Rehman.
8	Waqt	B.R. Chopra	Sunil Dutt, Sadhana, Raj Kumar, Sharmila Tagore, Shashi Kapoor, Balraj Sahni
9	Aradhana	Shakti Samanta	Rajesh Khanna, Sharmila Tagore
10	Do Raaste	Raj Khosla	Rajesh Khanna, Mumtaz

Top Actors

Heroes

1 Shammi Kapoor
2 Rajendra Kumar
3 Biswajeet
4 Joy Mukherjee
5 Manoj Kumar

Heroines

1 Nutan
2 Asha Parekh
3 Waheeda Rehman
4 Sadhana
5 Mala Sinha

Above: Shammi Kapoor and Saira Banu in *Junglee*.

Facing page: (left) Rajendra Kumar in *Sangam*;
Rajesh Khanna and Sharmila Tagore in *Aradhana*.

Top 10 Flops

	Movie	Director	Cast
1	Shaher Aur Sapna	K.A. Abbas	Dilip Raj, Surekha
2	Chitralekha	Kidar Sharma	Ashok Kumar, Meena Kumari
3	Door Gagan Ki Chaon Mein	Kishore Kumar	Kishore Kumar, Supriya Chowdhary
4	Yaadein	Sunil Dutt	Sunil Dutt, Nargis
5	Dil Diya Dard Liya	A.R. Kardar	Dilip Kumar, Waheeda Rehman
6	Teesri Kasam	Basu Bhattacharya	Raj Kapoor, Waheeda Rehman
7	Sangharsh	H.S. Rawail	Dilip Kumar, Vyjanthimala
8	Aakhri Khat	Chetan Anand	Rajesh Khanna, Master Bunty, Indrani Mukherjee
9	Mera Naam Joker	Raj Kapoor	Raj Kapoor, Dharmendra, Manoj Kumar, Rishi Kapoor, Rajendra Kumar, Simi Garewal, Padmini
10	Satyakam	Hrishikesh Mukherjee	Ashok Kumar, Dharmendra, Sharmila Tagore

Top 10 Hits

	Movie	Director	Cast
1	Bobby	Raj Kapoor	Rishi Kapoor, Dimple Kapadia
2	Haathi Mere Saathi	Chinappa Devar	Rajesh Khanna, Tanuja
3	Pakeezah	Kamal Amrohi	Ashok Kumar, Meena Kumari, Raj Kumar
4	Yaadon Ki Baraat	Nasir Husain	Dharmendra, Zeenat Aman, Tariq, Vijay Arora
5	.Zanjeer	Prakash Mehra	Amitabh Bachchan, Jaya Bhaduri, Pran
6	Deewaar	Yash Chopra	Amitabh Bachchan, Shashi Kapoor, Parveen Babi, Neetu Singh, Nirupa Roy
7	Jai Santoshi Maa	Vijay Sharma	Kanan Kaushal, Anita Guha, Ashish Kumar
8	Johnny Mera Naam	Vijay Anand	Dev Anand, Hema Malini
9	Roti Kapda Aur Makan	Manoj Kumar	Manoj Kumar, Zeenat Aman, Shashi Kapoor, Amitabh Bachchan, Moushumi Chatterjee
10	Sholay	Ramesh Sippy	Amitabh Bachchan, Jaya Bhaduri, Hema Malini, Sanjeev Kumar, Dharmendra

Top 10 Flops

	Movie	Director	Cast
1	Reshma Aur Shera	Sunil Dutt	Sunil Dutt, Waheeda Rehman, Raakhee, Amitabh Bachchan.
2	Joshila	Yash Chopra	Dev Anand, Hema Malini, Raakhee.
3	Imaan Dharam	Desh Mukherjee	Amitabh Bachchan, Rekha, Shashi Kapoor, Aparna Sen
4	Satyam Shivam Sundaram	Raj Kapoor	Shashi Kapoor, Zeenat Aman
5	Ishq Ishq Ishq	Dev Anand	Dev Anand, Zeenat Aman, Shabana Azmi
6	Shalimar	Krishna Shah	Dharmendra, Zeenat Aman
7	Mehbooba	Shakti Samanta	Rajesh Khanna, Hema Malini
8	The Burning Train	B.R. Chopra	Dharmendra, Hema Malini, Vinod Khanna, Parveen Babi
9	Dastaan	B.R. Chopra	Dilip Kumar, Sharmila Tagore
10	Chandi Sona	Sanjay Khan	Sanjay Khan, Parveen Babi

Right: Amitabh Bachchan in *Zanjeer*.

Facing page: Dharmendra and Mumtaz (left); Amjad Khan (right).

Top Actors

	Heroes		Heroines
1	Rajesh Khanna	1	Hema Malini
2	Amitabh Bachchan	2	Jaya Bhaduri
3	Dharmendra	3	Zeenat Aman
4	Jeetendra	4	Mumtaz
5	Vinod Khanna	5	Sharmila Tagore

1980s

Top 10 Hits

	Movie	Director	Cast
1	Ek Duuje Ke Liye	K. Balachander	Kamal Haasan, Rati Agnihotri
2	Qurbani	Feroz Khan	Feroz Khan, Zeenat Aman, Vinod Khanna
3	Naseeb	Manmohan Desai	Amitabh Bachchan, Hema Malini, Rishi Kapoor, Reena Roy
4	Coolie	Manmohan Desai	Amitabh Bachchan, Rati Agnihotri, Rishi Kapoor.
5	Hero	Subhash Ghai	Jackie Shroff, Meenakshi Sheshadri
6	Ram Teri Ganga Maili	Raj Kapoor	Mandakini, Rajiv Kapoor
7	Mr India	Shekhar Kapur	Sridevi, Anil Kapoor
8	Qayamat Se Qayamat Tak	Mansoor Khan	Aamir Khan, Juhi Chawla
9	Tezaab	N. Chandra	Anil Kapoor, Madhuri Dixit
10	Chandni	Yash Chopra	Sridevi, Rishi Kapoor, Vinod Khanna
11	Maine Pyar Kiya	Sooraj Barjatya	Bhagyashree, Salman Khan

Top Actors

Heroes
1 Amitabh Bachchan
2 Jeetendra
3 Dharmendra

Heroines
1 Rekha
2 Sridevi
3 Padmini Kolhapure
4 Zeenat Aman
5 Rati Agnihotri

Right: Sridevi.

Below: A scene from *Ram Teri Ganga Maili*

Facing page: Hema Malini (left) and Anil Kapoor

Top 10 Flops

	Movie	Director	Cast
1	Deedar-e-Yaar	H.S. Rawail	Jeetendra, Tina Munim, Rishi Kapoor
2	Razia Sultan	Kamal Amrohi	Dharmendra, Hema Malini
3	Silsila	Yash Chopra	Amitabh Bachchan, Rekha, Jaya Bhaduri; Shashi Kapoor, Sanjeev Kumar
4	Sagar	Ramesh Sippy	Kamal Haasan, Dimple Kapadia, Rishi Kapoor
5	Sultanat	Mukul Anand	Dharmendra, Sunny Deol, Sridevi, Juhi Chawla
6	Hathyar	J.P. Dutta	Sanjay Dutt, Amrita Singh, Rishi Kapoor, Dharmendra
7	Vijay	Yash Chopra	Rajesh Khanna, Hema Malini, Anil Kapoor, Meenakshi Sheshadri
8	Mahaan	S. Ramnathan	Amitabh Bachchan, Waheeda Rehman, Zeenat Aman
9	Ek Nayi Paheli	K. Balachander	Raj Kumar, Hema Malini, Kamal Haasan, Padmini Kolhapure
10	Shakti	Ramesh Sippy	Dilip Kumar, Amitabh Bachchan, Raakhee, Smita Patil

Below: Shah Rukh Khan in *Dilwale Dulhaniya Le Jayenge.*

Right: Madhuri Dixit and Salman Khan in *Hum Aapke Hain Koun.*

Facing page: Aishwarya Rai in *Hum Dil De Chuke Sanam.*

Top 10 Hits

	Movie	Director	Cast
1	Dilwale Dulhaniya Le Jayenge	Aditya Chopra	Shah Rukh Khan, Kajol, Amrish Puri, Anupam Kher
2	Hum Aapke Hain Koun	Sooraj Barjatya	Salman Khan, Madhuri Dixit
3	Kuch Kuch Hota Hai	Karan Johar	Shah Rukh Khan, Kajol, Rani Mukherjee, Salman Khan
4	Ashiqui	Mahesh Bhatt	Anu Aggarwal, Rahul Roy
5	Rangeela	Ram Gopal Varma	Aamir Khan, Urmila Matondkar, Jackie Shroff
6	Border	J.P. Dutta	Sunny Deol, Sunil Shetty, Akshaye Khanna, Jackie Shroff, Raakhee, Tabu
7	Raja Hindustani	Dharmesh Darshan	Aamir Khan, Karisma Kapoor
8	Hum Dil De Chuke Sanam	Sanjay Leela Bhansali	Salman Khan, Aishwarya Rai, Ajay Devgan
9	Darr	Yash Chopra	Shah Rukh Khan, Sunny Deol, Juhi Chawla
10	Karan Arjun	Rakesh Roshan	Shah Rukh Khan, Salman Khan, Kajol, Mamta Kulkarni

Top 10 Flops

	Movie	Director	Cast
1	Lamhe	Yash Chopra	Anil Kapoor, Sridevi
2	Dil Se	Mani Ratnam	Shah Rukh Khan, Manisha Koirala, Preity Zinta
3	1942: A Love Story	Vidhu Vinod Chopra	Anil Kapoor, Mnaisha Koirala
4	Khamoshi: The Musical	Sanjay Leela Bhansali	Nana Patekar, Manisha Koirala, Salman Khan, Seema Biswas
5	Trimurti	Mukul Anand	Anil Kapoor, Shah Rukh Khan, Jackie Shroff, Gautami, Priya Tendulkar
6	Roop Ki Rani Choron Ka Raja	Satish Kaushik	Sridevi, Anil Kapoor, Jackie Shroff
7	Ajooba	Shashi Kapoor	Amitabh Bachchan, Dimple Kapadia, Rishi Kapoor
8	Mrityudaata	Mehul Kumar	Amitabh Bachchan, Dimple Kapadia, Karisma Kapoor
9	Parampara	Yash Chopra	Aamir Khan, Saif Ali Khan, Raveena Tandon
10	Kshatriya	J.P. Dutta	Dharmendra, Sunny Deol, Sanjay Dutt, Raveena Tandon, Raakhee

Top Actors

	Heroes		Heroines
1	Shah Rukh Khan	1	Madhuri Dixit
2	Amitabh Bachchan	2	Karisma Kapoor
3	Sunny Deol.	3	Kajol
4	Aamir Khan	4	Manisha Koirala
5	Salman Khan	5	Raveena Tandon

2000s

Top 5 Hits

	Movie	Director	Cast
1	Lagaan	Ashutosh Gowariker	Aamir Khan, Gracy Singh
2	Gadar: Ek Prem Kahani	Anil Sharma	Sunny Deol, Amisha Patel
3	Kaho Na...Pyar Hai	Rakesh Roshan	Hrithik Roshan, Amisha Patel
4	Devdas	Sanjay Leela Bhansali	Shah Rukh Khan, Madhuri Dixit, Aishwarya Rai
5	Baghban	Ravi Chopra	Amitabh Bachchan, Hema Malini, Salman Khan, Nakul Vaid

Left: Kareena Kapoor and Hrithik Roshan in *Main Prem Ki Diwani Hoon.*

Right: Madhuri Dixit in *Devdas.*

Facing page: Preity Zinta in *Mission Kashmir.*

Top Actors

Heroes

1 Shah Rukh Khan
2 Amitabh Bachchan
3 Hrithik Roshan
4 Salman Khan
5 Aamir Khan

Heroines

1 Aishwarya Rai
2 Rani Mukherjee
3 Preity Zinta.
4 Kareena Kapoor
5 Sushmita Sen

Top 5 Flops

	Movie	Director	Cast
1	Main Prem Ki Diwani Hoon	Sooraj Barjatya	Kareena Kapoor, Hrithik Roshan, Abhishek Bachchan.
2	LOC	J.P. Dutta	Sanjay Dutt, Abhishek Bachchan, Akshaye Khanna, Ajay Devgan, Manoj Bajpai, Kareena Kapoor, Raveena Tandon, Esha Deol
3	Kisna	Subhash Ghai	Vivek Oberoi, Isha Shravani
4	Boom	Kaizad Gustad	Amitabh Bachchan, Zeenat Aman, Jackie Shroff, Katrina Kaif
5	Lakshya	Farhan Akhtar	Amitabh Bachchan, Hrithik Roshan, Preity Zinta

Index

Chopra, Aditya, 29, 132, 133, 168
Chopra, B.R., 102, 114, 122, 123, 160, 162, 165
Chopra, Prem, 39, 42, 52, 126
Chopra, Vidhu Vinod, 75, 74, 131, 169
Chopra, Yash, 18, 53, 58, 59, 76, 122, 124, 127, 129, 164, 165, 166, 167, 168, 169
Chotisi Baat, 56, 100
Chowdhary, Ranjit, 82, 148
Chowdhury, Jehangir, 155
Chowdhury, Salil, 12, 44, 122, 144
Chunilal, Rai Bahadur, 33
Chupke Chupke, 56, 67, 101
Company, 142
Coolie, 75, 117, 166
Cuckoo, 10
Daag, 52
Dacait, 82, 140
Daera, 11, 19, 161
Damini, 79, 92
Das, Nandita, 82, 88, 156
Das, Vasundhara, 136
Dastak, 41, 54, 100, 102
David, 12
De, Dipankar, 151
Deewaar, 56, 58
Denzongpa, Danny, 48, 61, 128, 137
Deo, Ramesh, 37, 44
Deo, Seema, 44
Deol, Esha, 95, 134, 171
Deol, Sunny, 79, 112, 124, 140, 141, 167, 168, 1689, 170
Desai, Manmohan, 61, 117, 142, 166
Desai, Nitin C., 138
Desai, Vasant, 15, 36, 46, 110
Dev, Rahul, 137
Devdas, 11, 14, 15, 21, 22, 43, 51, 64, 65, 78, 81, 93, 96, 144, 153, 170
Devgan, Ajay, 95, 131, 133, 142, 168, 171
Dharmaraj, Rabindra, 148
Dharmendra, 24, 29, 30, 31, 32, 40, 41, 46, 47, 54, 60, 72, 101, 111, 112, 140, 163, 164, 165, 166, 167, 169
Dhawan, Anil, 100
Dhawan, David, 103
Dhawan, Prem, 14, 42
Dholakia, Rajat, 154
Dhool Ka Phool, 18, 19, 24

Dil Chahta Hai, 77, 92, 137
Dil Kya Kare, 126
Dil Se, 80, 81, 85, 111, 169
Dil Tera Deewana, 155
Dillagi, 154
Dilwale Dulhania Le Jayenge, 100, 132, 133, 168
Diwedi, Dr Chandraprakash, 94
Dixit, Madhuri, 75, 91, 93, 117, 166, 168, 169, 170
Do Aankhen Bara Haath, 15, 22, 64
Do Badan, 63
Do Bigha Zameen, 12, 19, 39, 57, 81, 137
Do Raaste, 39, 40, 162
Doosra Aadmi, 62
Dr Kotnis Ki Amar Kahani, 14, 15, 44, 110, 131
Drohkaal, 80, 96
Dulari, 50
Dulhan Wohi Jo Piya Man Bhaye, 60, 102, 103
Durbar, Ismail, 93, 133
Dutt, Geeta (Roy), 18, 25, 55, 96
Dutt, Guru, 16, 18, 19, 24, 25, 55, 76, 98, 111, 161
Dutt, Sanjay, 114, 140, 167, 169, 171
Dutt, Sunil, 16, 19, 26, 27, 34, 49, 61, 99, 114, 160, 162, 163, 165
Dutt, Utpal, 46, 103
Dutta, J.P., 72, 112, 140, 167, 168, 169, 171
Dutta, N., 18
Ehsan, 92
Ek Bar Phir, 65, 146
Ek Doctor Ki Maut, 76, 87
Ek Duuje Ke Liye, 69, 128, 166
Ek Pal, 82, 155
Faasla, 145
Faraaz, 94
Fire, 82, 88, 103
Fiza, 89, 131
Gandhi, 118
Gandhi, Indira, 57, 84, 106
Ganga Jumna, 23, 26, 27, 162
Ganguly, Anil, 56
Garam Hawa, 39, 52, 53
Garewal, Simi, 45, 47, 54, 65, 127, 163
Ghai, Subash, 65, 132, 166, 171
Ghatak, Ritwik, 17, 80
Ghayal, 87, 141

Ghose, Gautam, 154
Ghulami, 72, 80
Gidwani, Kitu, 88
Godbole, Shrirang, 157
Godmother, 88, 122
Gokhale, Vikram, 133
Golmaal, 65, 103
Gopalkrishnan, Adoor, 93
Gossain, Ravi, 84
Goswami, Bindiya, 103
Gowarikar, Ashutosh, 137, 138
Guddi, 46, 47
Guha, Anita, 38, 164
Guide, 30, 31, 35, 76, 111, 157, 162
Gulzar, 24, 36, 40, 44, 46, 48, 49, 50, 51, 57, 58, 60, 62, 68, 70, 72, 73, 78, 84, 85, 87, 89, 94, 103, 104, 108, 112, 116, 123, 137, 151, 155
Gulzar, Raakhee, (see Raakhee)
Gumrah, 30, 114
Gunaji, Milind, 88
Gupta, Neena, 106
Haasan, Kamal, 70, 108, 128, 136, 166, 167
Hallauri, Khurshid, 75
Hangal, A.K., 46, 56
Hansraj, Jugal, 116, 117
Haqeeqat, 30, 111
Hare Rama, Hare Krishna, 50, 51, 144
Hareesh, 131
Hari, 76, 124, 129
Hashmat, M.G., 56
Hathyar, 85, 112, 140, 167
Hattangadi, Rohini, 150, 152
Hazaar Chaurasi Ki Maa, 107, 156
Hazarika, Bhupen, 78, 155
Helen, 33, 83, 133
Henna, 88, 130
Hera Pheri, 58, 132
Hey Ram!, 131, 136
Howrah Bridge, 99
Hum Aapke Hain Kaun, 96, 117, 168
Hum Dil De Chuke Sanam, 93, 123, 133, 168
Hum Dono, 27, 110, 111
Hum Kisise Kum Nahin, 60, 65, 129
Hunterwali, 147
Husain, Anwar, 30
Husain, Nasir, 33, 65, 74, 164
Hussein, Nazmul, 37
Iftekhar, 103

Ijaazat, 73, 82
Ilaiyaraja, 70, 116, 136
Indivar, 35, 37, 42, 43, 141
Insaaf Ka Tarazu, 69
Irani Faredoon, 10
Irani, Ardeshir, 19
Irani, Aruna, 35, 126
Ittefaq, 40, 122, 123
Jaane Bhi Do Yaaron, 75, 106
Jaffrey, Saeed, 72, 104, 105, 130, 150
Jaffri, Javed, 82
Jagte Raho, 14, 22, 59, 161
Jai Santoshi Maa, 57, 104, 164
Jaidev, 26, 49, 110, 128
Jaikishan (see Shankar-Jaikishan)
Jain, Indu, 104, 105, 152
Jain, Madan, 152, 153
Jain, Ravindra, 72, 102, 103, 130
Jaipuri, Hasrat, 13, 21, 28, 32, 45, 47, 72
Jalal, Farida, 38, 58, 86, 118, 126, 130, 132
Jamuna, 22, 34, 51
Jatin-Lalit, 77, 83, 86, 118, 132
Jayant, 10, 36, 39, 111
Jaykar, Smita, 157
Jayshree, 110
Jeetendra, 42, 43, 51, 58, 115, 165, 166, 167
Jewel Thief, 36, 121
Jhansi Ki Rani, 52, 56
Jhulka, Ayesha, 77, 108
Jis Desh Mein Ganga Behti Hai, 21, 26
Jo Jeeta Wohi Sikandar, 77, 91
Johar, Karan, 86, 87, 118, 127, 133, 168
Johnny Mera Naam, 164
Joshi, Sharman, 88
Julie, 57, 126
Junglee, 33, 80, 162, 163
Junoon, 63, 66, 136
Kabhi Kabhie, 58, 124, 127
Kabhi Khushi Kabhie Gham, 118, 127, 132
Kagaz Ke Phool, 65, 76, 161
Kaho Na... Pyar Hai, 90, 91, 132, 170
Kajol, 55, 86, 118, 131, 132, 168, 169
Kala Bazaar, 21
Kalyanji-Anandji, 37, 42, 43, 56, 64
Kalyug, 66, 69
Kamal, Raj, 104, 105